The Fa

G000123776

The Faithful Parent

A BIBLICAL GUIDE TO RAISING A FAMILY

Martha Peace and Stuart W. Scott

P&R PUBLISHING
P.O. BOX 817 • PHILLIPSBURG • NEW JERSEY 08865-0817

Unless otherwise indicated, Scripture quotations are from The Holy Bible, English Standard Version, copyright © 2001 by Crossway Bibles, a division of Good News Publishers. Used by permission. All rights reserved.

Scripture quotations marked (NASB) are from the *New American Standard Bible*®. © Copyright The Lockman Foundation 1960, 1962, 1963, 1968, 1971, 1972, 1973, 1975, 1977. Used by permission. Printed in the United States of America

Library of Congress Cataloging-in-Publication Data

Peace, Martha.
  The faithful parent : a biblical guide to raising a family / Martha Peace and Stuart W. Scott.
       p. cm.
  Includes bibliographical references.
  ISBN 978-1-59638-201-5 (pbk.)
  1. Child rearing–Religious aspects–Christianity. 2. Child rearing–Biblical teaching.
  I. Scott, Stuart, 1955- II. Title.
  BV4529.P42 2010
  248.8'45–dc22

                              2010008346

Stuart dedicates this book to:
his beloved parents,
Raymond and Anne Scott—
Raymond, who is in the presence of Jesus, and Anne,
who is still serving our Lord with us—
and to his children,
Christa and Marc,
who are a gift from God
and whom he dearly loves

Martha dedicates this book to:
her beloved grandchildren,
Nathan, Tommy, Jordan, Kelsey, Caleb,
Cameron, Kaylyn, Carter, Matthew,
Kylee, Noah, and Emma.

Contents

Part Three: The Persevering Parent

Foreword

Arriving one afternoon at a venue where I would be speaking to parents about shepherding their children, I was met at the door by a frantic mom.

"I am so glad I bumped into you. I need help. My four-year-old asked me last night, 'Mommy, why should I have to obey you, you never obey me?' You have to help me, Dr. Tripp; I didn't know how to answer him."

There is a simple answer to this preschooler's question, "Honey, God says that children should obey their mommy but he does not tell mommies to obey their children."

The confusion in this young mom, the lack of a ready-made answer to this basic question, has reached critical mass in the church. Parents are concerned and, like this young mom, almost frantic for solid biblical answers.

Other Christian parents are confused as well. "How do I correct and discipline my child who lies when he could just as well have told the truth?" "My son throws tantrums at the most inopportune times, in the doctor's office, in the supermarket. What do I do?" "I know my 14-year-old is too old to spank, but what can I do to discipline him?" "My child just won't talk to me; I can never get beyond one-word answers."

"How do I keep my teen from spending hours playing games on the computer?" "How can I get beyond my own anger so I can correct in godly and constructive ways?"

The confusion is easy to understand. In the simplest of times, raising children is an overwhelming task. These are not the simplest of times. Many voices are giving competing and often contradictory messages. Our families are confronted with ubiquitous media that are shaping the structure of family life more than we know. We are raising children in hectic times when our schedules are stretched and life is moving apace. We don't seem to have enough time with our children, and when we do we are not sure what to do with it.

The need of the hour is the timeless clarity and wisdom of the Word of God. The Bible is robust, providing solid counsel, tailor-made for every era and culture. The greatest need of parents is biblical knowledge coupled with the wisdom and understanding needed to break down the application of Scripture into sensible and doable training and nurture of children.

The Faithful Parent: A Biblical Guide to Raising a Family provides the comprehensive help that parents need. Martha Peace and Stuart Scott have done for parenting what their earlier books did for the roles of a husband and a wife.

Part One of *The Faithful Parent* lays a solid foundation in the Word of God. It begins with a brief exposition of what it means to bring up children in the discipline and instruction of the Lord (Eph. 6:4). They show how discipline is providing structures, restraint, and even correction, while instruction is developing the mind-set and heart-set to think biblically about all aspects of life.

The next course of this foundation shows the child's twin callings in Ephesians 6:1–3 both to obey and to honor father and mother.

The final course of the foundation is an insightfully wise discussion of salvation and sanctification of a child.

The temptation of many in picking up this book will be to turn to the section or sections that describe their children's developmental stages and immediately begin reading there. If you do, you will find practical help and guidance, but you will miss the essential foundations that will enable you to build into your family life a solid structure of biblical parenting.

Part Two tackles the various child-rearing stages: infants, toddlers, preschoolers, school-age children, and the feared teenage years. For each of these developmental stages, Peace and Scott have identified the physical and conceptual maturity, along with the appropriate expectations parents may have. To this they have added the implications and application of tailoring discipline and instruction in the Lord in an age-appropriate manner.

This main body of the book makes it more than a guide for developing biblical perspectives. This is a valuable reference tool for all developmental stages. What you may expect of your children, what they should expect from you, and even valuable tips and pointers make this book one that parents will want to keep on the nightstand or in a convenient spot in the most-used room of the house.

My experience is that many Christian parents who love their children and desire good for them can be blind to ways they provoke their children to anger. Part Two describes fifteen ways that parents can unwittingly provoke their children. These provocations will be familiar to anyone who has spent much time counseling parents and children. Since none of us are perfect parents, you will find yourself in this chapter at least once or twice.

Part Three addresses special cases that I find raised frequently by parents when I teach about shepherding the hearts of children. What about blended families, single parents, families with shared custody, parents who share children with unbelieving spouses, or special-needs children? These cases are taken up and interpreted through the lens of the discipline and instruction of the Lord.

Most parents will get to the end of this excellent volume looking for more. And there is more! There are several appendices that round out the message of the book.

I always look for two things in a parenting book: (1) I look for insight and understanding of the heart as the wellspring of life. (2) I look for the book to be full of the hope and grace of the gospel. Both of these are here in abundance. I am thankful that concern for internal motivation and gospel empowerment are not separate chapters in this book. They are rather threads of truth woven throughout the fabric of each chapter. And gospel hope is present as essential truth not only for children, but as it ought to be, for parents as well.

The book you are holding is an outstanding resource. The authors are seasoned Christians who are safe spiritual guides. They are full of the hope and grace of the gospel. They are wise in their understanding of the nature of the Christian life. They are insightful in their understanding of the needs of children and the difficulties of being a faithful parent. They are mature in their application of the Bible and its message to the challenges of raising children. This will be a timeless resource for faithful parents.

Tedd Tripp

Acknowledgments

We are very grateful to Martha's childhood friend and next-door neighbor, Dr. Andrea Starrett. Andrea, a neurodevelopmental pediatrician, lives and has practiced medicine in New Orleans. She contributed several valuable suggestions that were used to strengthen the growth and development sections as well as the chapter on special cases. Her expertise was obvious. Thank you, Andrea!

We also want to give special thanks to Dr. Laura Hendrickson. Laura formerly practiced as a psychiatrist and is currently a biblical counselor in San Diego. Laura gave us permission to adapt her material in the book, *When Good Kids Make Bad Choices*,[1] for the section of this book, "When the Child Has Special Needs." There was no way that we could have improved on her material. Thank you, Laura!

Zondra Scott, Stuart's wife, helped edit, made good suggestions, and managed to cook homemade biscuits for our breakfast one morning while we worked on the book at Stuart and Zondra's home in Louisville. She was a joy to be around

---

1. Elyse Fitzpatrick, Jim Newheiser, and Laura Hendrickson, *When Good Kids Make Bad Choices* (Eugene, OR: Harvest House, 2005).

and made the entire process go much smoother than it could have. Thank you, Zondra!

For sure we have to acknowledge Anna Peace Maupin. Anna is Martha's daughter and a homeschooling mom of seven kids. She was an English major gifted in writing and editing. In the midst of this project when Stuart and Martha lost all hope, Anna was confident it could be fixed. So she fixed it, and the Lord used her to restore hope to Stuart and Martha. Thank you, Anna!

A special blessing was John Crotts, Martha's pastor. Near the end of the project, John read the manuscript and had several major suggestions. He even had sort of an emergency meeting with us one morning at the Atlanta Bread Company restaurant. Well, both of us knew he was wise in his suggestions, although we moaned inwardly at the thought of additional work. After doing the additional work, we can say sincerely, Thank you, John!

Many thanks to Jan Haley and Barb Smith for their editorial suggestions. This book is much more readable as a result of their labors of love. Thank you, Jan and Barb!

Marvin Padgett from P&R Publishing was very enthusiastic about this project. Working with Marvin was a joy for us, and we hope it was for him. We also want to thank John Hughes for his editing and encouragement. Thank you, Marvin and John. You were both a blessing.

Of course, we are so very grateful to our Lord Jesus Christ. He has enabled us to persevere in this project. To him all glory is due, and our prayer is that he will use this book to help parents love and honor him more as they strive to bring their children up "in the discipline and instruction of the Lord" (Eph. 6:4).

Martha Peace and Stuart Scott

PART ONE

The Biblical Basis

But as for you, continue in what you have learned and have firmly believed, knowing from whom you learned it and how from childhood you have been acquainted with the sacred writings, which are able to make you wise for salvation through faith in Christ Jesus. All Scripture is breathed out by God and profitable for teaching, for reproof, for correction, and for training in righteousness, that the man of God may be competent, equipped for every good work. (2 Tim. 3:14–17)

The Goal of Parenting and One's Hope

In all of eternity, there has been only one perfectly faithful parent, and he had the only perfectly faithful son. Of course, we are talking about God the Father and the Lord Jesus Christ. They loved each other perfectly and never sinned. The Father was *always* pleased with the Son. The Son *always* carried out the will of the Father. Neither one would ever sin because they are holy. What a beautiful picture!

Now imagine a father driving his family on vacation with his wife in the passenger seat and their two children in the back seat. Suddenly, one of the children begins to scream, "He's looking at me!" Next, a free-for-all breaks out in the back seat. Everyone in the car is instantly unnerved and sinning in one or more ways. Not so beautiful a picture.

Parents and children need help, a lot of help. They need help from the one who is perfect, who does understand our need, and who helps us—God himself. That's what this book is about. *The Faithful Parent* gives a practical, biblical perspective about bringing children up "in the discipline and instruction of the Lord," through and because of God's grace to us (Eph. 6:4).[1] Our aims are to present the underlying biblical basis for this discipline and instruction, to give you a picture of every-day life with your children, and to challenge you to become a faithful parent who perseveres and leaves the results to God.

The Right Goal

The goal for the Christian parent is to be *faithful to God's Word by his grace and for his glory.* You see, in Christ we have the great hope that we can be faithful whether our children are faithful or not.

What does it mean to be faithful? The word "faithful" occurs many times in the Old and New Testaments. In the Old Testament, "faithful" is used to describe God. It means to be "permanent, true, certain, of long continuance, stead-fast, sure, trustworthy and carries the idea of a firm and sure support."[2] Similarly, in the New Testament, the word translated as "faithful" means "to be trusted, reliable, or true."[3] So, given what we learn about the word "faithful" in the Scriptures, if we are to be faithful parents we will be steadfast, trustworthy, and true concerning our commitment to God and his Word.

1. Unless noted otherwise, all Bible quotations are from the English Standard Version.

2. James Strong, *The New Strong's Concise Dictionary of the Words in the Hebrew Bible* (Nashville: Thomas Nelson, 1995), 10 (#539).

3. W. E. Vine, *Expository Dictionary of the New Testament* (Old Tappan, NJ: H. Revell, 1966), 72.

We will also be like God, reliable in our parental care and in our commitment to our children's good.

An example of parents' faithfulness is shown in the following story about Stuart and Zondra Scott's daughter, Christa, when she was three years old. She was to be a flower girl in her uncle's wedding. Her family traveled to a distant city for the wedding, and they stayed with Martha and Sanford's family. One of the Peace family members was their sixteen-year-old son David. David was a tall, rather skinny kid, who probably barely noticed the little girl. Christa, however, upon being introduced to David, was wide-eyed in wonder. With much excitement she told David's mother, "Come and see David. He killed Goliath!"

How much fun this was for everyone who was there that day! Even though Christa did not quite grasp the huge historical time gap, it was obvious that she had been taught Bible stories and that she believed with all her little heart that they were true. Stuart and Zondra were being *faithful* to teach Christa about the Lord and his Word.

Faithfulness, not perfection, is rewarded by the Lord. That's because we can no more live a sinless life than we can make our children do the same thing. Only our Lord Jesus is he "who knew no sin" (2 Cor. 5:21). He never sinned, but we do, and he knew we would need his help and encouragement to raise our children faithfully as he desires. The astounding good news is that by God's grace Christian parents have been placed in a position where they *can* learn and obey God's will more and more, because they have God's Spirit indwelling them. A person who is striving to honor the Lord in parenting, repenting, and changing is a faithful parent. Although we will not be perfect parents, we can, day-by-day, learn to live out

5

God's instructions. Some day, we *can* hear the Lord say to us what the master told his slave, "Well done, good and faithful servant" (Matt. 25:21).

How can we know whether we are faithfully living out God's instruction? We know it when we are seeking to live habitually according to God's Word. The Scriptures are God's revealed will to us (Deut. 29:29; 2 Tim. 3:16–17). God himself speaks to us directly through the Bible. The Bible is unlike any other book, because it is God's Word. Therefore, it is sufficient to tell us what we need to know to parent faithfully.

The Scriptures don't give us step-by-step details on every decision a parent makes. They do, however, provide truth in the form of direct commands or principles for us to follow. For example, a general principle would be "Trust in the LORD with all your heart, and do not lean on your own understanding" (Prov. 3:5).

The Scriptures also tell us about the Lord Jesus Christ and how to become a Christian. Second Timothy 3:15 tells us that "the sacred writings . . . are able to make you wise for salvation through faith in Christ Jesus." So, parents can live out God's Word faithfully only if they are, first of all, born-again believers.[4]

Once we are saved, God begins the work of sanctification in our lives. The root word for *sanctification* in the original Greek has the underlying meaning of being *holy*.[5] This is a process of spiritual growth that begins at the moment of your salvation and will be completed in heaven (Titus 2:11–14). Our children are often one of the main means that God uses to show

4. For more information about how to become a Christian, see Appendix A.
5. James Strong, *The New Strong's Concise Dictionary of the Words in the Greek Testament* (Nashville: Thomas Nelson, 1995), 1 (# 38).

us our sin and mold us more and more into his likeness. It is common to hear a young mother say, "I did not know I had an anger problem until I had children!" So, in order to help overcome sinful tendencies and make us more like Christ, the Lord Jesus prayed to the Father on our behalf, "Sanctify them in the truth; *your word* is truth" (John 17:17, emphasis added). We as parents must keep in mind that our children are not the only ones in the sanctification process.

So far we have seen that the parent's goal is to be *faithful to God's Word*, but certainly there is more. The only way we *can* be faithful is *by his grace*. God's grace is his unmerited favor and help toward his children who are fallen and hopeless on their own. This grace is available through the person of Jesus Christ who provided salvation for those who believe in him. God's grace is over all his creation in a general way, but also enables his children to be more like the Lord Jesus on a daily basis. Although we do not deserve it, God has supernaturally gifted us with the motivation and the strength to do his will. Although we have the responsibility to "work out [our] salvation with fear and trembling," it is "God who works in [us], both to will and to work for his good pleasure" (Phil. 2:12–13, adaptation added).

Certainly, we are to prayerfully strive to obey, but it is only by God's grace helping us that anything good and pleasing comes out of our lives. At times, parenting can be a rather daunting task, but God's enabling grace is always available and sufficient because, "His divine power has granted to us all things that pertain to life and godliness, through the knowledge of him who called us to his own glory and excellence . . . ." (2 Peter 1:3). With God's help we can be more consistent in our training and instructing in love. It doesn't take a parent long to realize that it takes great patience and perseverance to work with children, but all the grace we need is available. We may have old thinking and old parental habits that need to be renewed, but God *is* able to help us change as we do our part and prayerfully depend on him.

One young mother we know is a new Christian who has struggled with anger and impatience, especially toward her seven-year-old son. It seems that her son often felt the brunt of her mood-of-the-day. His mom was convicted that she was being unkind, and she began confessing her sin to God and her little boy. She also began to rethink her thoughts when she was tempted to respond in anger. One day in the kitchen of their home, her son did something that would normally have sent her into orbit. That day, however, was different. The Lord enabled her to think, "Love is patient. I can show love to him in spite of his sin." She responded to her son with loving discipline and with joy as she realized that God was helping her to become a loving Christian mother.

Change must begin with the parent. In Deuteronomy 6:6, God tells parents, "these words that I command you today shall be on your heart." Our children need to see in our own lives daily what we want to see in theirs. The Lord can give us grace on the spot to refrain from sharp reproof and hurtful words. He can keep growing us so we can be more and more faithful to bring him glory.

Because it is only by God's grace that we are enabled to renew our minds and be more like God, God gets all the credit. In other words, he gets the glory. God's glory involves the display of *his* beautiful perfections (sometimes accompanied in the Scriptures by brightness, Ex. 33:18–23). To glorify God is to give him the honor, literally "the weight," due his perfections.[6] This beauty of God's perfections is to be reflected in all Christians' lives as they live obedient to his Word in the power of the Holy Spirit. Because of what God has done in us through Jesus Christ, there is nothing, however mundane, that we cannot do for his glory. We like to think of it as being a "living sacrifice" for the Lord (Rom. 12:1). The apostle Paul explained what it means to glorify God in clear, practical terms: "So, whether you eat or drink, or whatever you do, do *all* to the glory of God" (1 Cor. 10:31, emphasis added).

All includes faithfully fulfilling the biblical responsibilities of a parent. Parents have two primary biblical responsibilities toward their children, to bring them up: (1) in the discipline of the Lord, and (2) in the instruction of the Lord.

Your Basic Biblical Responsibilities as a Parent

> Fathers, do not provoke your children to anger, but bring them up in the discipline and instruction of the Lord. (Eph. 6:4)

The Greek word for discipline in this verse is *paideia*, which has the basic idea of training one's external life.[7] This is a broad term that encompasses some sort of structured guidance and restraint, whether by practical guidelines for living, encouragement, reproof, or chastisement (for either disobedience and/or sinful attitudes and, of course, as appropriate

6. The Hebrew word for glory is *kavod*, meaning weight, splendor, or copiousness. Strong, *Words in the Hebrew Bible*, 62 (#3519).

7. Gerhard Kittel, Gerhard Friedrich, and Geoffrey W. Bromiley, eds., *Theological Dictionary of the New Testament: Abridged in One Volume* (Grand Rapids: Eerdmans, 1985), 753–58.

for the age of the child). Instruction, on the other hand, is the Greek word *nouthesia*, which means to "place or set in the mind."[8] The idea here is addressing one's internal mind/ heart. The parents are to teach their children (as faithfully as the parents can) to think biblically about God, man, Satan, the world, and life.

For example, we must teach our children what it means to fear and love God (Prov. 1:7 and Matt. 22:37–40). They need to understand that their lives are, first of all, about a relationship with God. Living in a Christian home should facilitate honor and respect of a worthy God and encourage wholehearted delight and allegiance toward him. As you demonstrate that you love God with all your heart, it will be easier to find examples of God's faithfulness and ways to give him the love and honor he deserves.

While teaching and disciplining their children, parents are not to provoke them to anger. This principle is expressed in a slightly different way in Colossians 3.

> Fathers, do not provoke your children, lest they become discouraged. (Col. 3:21)

Every parent has at some time or another unnecessarily provoked a child, but this verse is referring to an ongoing, habitual activity. Often parents are bigger, stronger, and more coordinated, and they know more than their children. In this case, it is easy to provoke children to wrath by demanding more than the children are capable of accomplishing. Other ways that parents provoke their children are by being cruel, making fun

8. Walter Bauer, *A Greek-English Lexicon of the New Testament and Other Early Christian Literature*, 2nd ed., ed. F. Wilbur Gingrich and Frederick W. Danker (Chicago: University of Chicago Press, 1979), 544–45.

of their children, reacting in a harsh way, overreacting when disciplining children, withholding love, or not expressing joy in them.[9] The Scriptures are clear about protecting those of whom we can easily take advantage, and that includes children. So instead of provoking them to anger, parents have *two* responsibilities toward their children, to bring them up in (1) the discipline of the Lord, and (2) the instruction of the Lord.

Parents are not the only ones in a family who can glorify God through being faithful. If the child is a Christian, he or she can do so, too. Like their parents, children have two basic biblical responsibilities: (1) to obey their parents, and (2) to honor their parents.

Basic Biblical Responsibilities of the Child

"Children, obey your parents in the Lord, for this is right." (Eph. 6:1)

Children are to obey their parents unless a parent asks them to sin. We find the command *obey your parents* clearly stated in Ephesians 6:1, but it is qualified by God. They are to obey "in the Lord, for this is right." The Lord would never ask them to sin and neither, of course, should the parent. In addition, Acts 5:28–29 makes it clear that those in authority do not have the right to ask those under them to sin. Peter explained to his own authorities that "we must obey God rather

9. For a more thorough study on ways parents provoke children to anger, we recommend Lou Priolo's book, *The Heart of Anger* (Amityville, NY: Calvary Press, 1997), 29–51.

than men!" when a ruler's requirement conflicted with God's. God is always the highest authority.

The Greek word for "obey" is *hupakouo*.[10] This is a compound word made up of *hupa* ("to be under") and *akouo* ("to listen" or "to hear"). We derive our English word "acoustic" from *akouo*. Acoustic is "relating to the sense or organs of hearing, to sound, or to the science of sounds."[11] So, the responsibility of the child is to listen, *akouo*, to his parents' instruction with the *intent* of obeying. The reason being, the child is under, *hupa*, the parents' authority.

Obedience leads logically to the second basic responsibility of the child.

> "Honor your father and mother" (this is the first commandment with a promise), "that it may go well with you and that you may live long in the land." (Eph. 6:2–3)

When this commandment was given, it included a beautiful promise of a long life. As a child obeyed, he would live well and longer, especially since the result of rebellion was stoning. In his letter to the Ephesians, God through Paul is highlighting how important and beneficial it is for a child to honor his parents. Indeed, a child honors his parents when he speaks *about* them and *to* them in a gracious, respectful way, and when he seeks to submit to his parents' authority while in their home.

So far we have seen that children are under the authority of their parents and that children have two responsibilities: (1) to obey their parents, and (2) to honor their parents. We

10. Strong, *Words in the Greek Testament*, 10 (#5219).
11. G. & C. Merriam Company, *Merriam-Webster Dictionary* (Boston: G. K. Hall, 1977), 26.

have also seen that for God's glory and by his grace, parents can faithfully fulfill their two basic responsibilities: (1) to discipline their children, and (2) to instruct them in things pertaining to the Lord.

Our Hope

Each child whom God gives us is a special blessing from him. He blesses us not only with the child but also with the promise that when we need help, we can always "with confidence draw near to the throne of grace, that we may receive mercy and find grace to help in time of need" (Heb. 4:16). God has promised that *he* is "faithful, and he will not let you be tempted beyond your ability . . ." (1 Cor. 10:13).

We have great hope not only in God's provision of daily grace to help us, but also from the help that is in God's Word. The Bible was, among other reasons, "written for our instruction, that through endurance and through the encouragement of the Scriptures we might have hope" (Rom. 15:4). A recent television commercial claimed that "children do not come with an instruction manual." Well, that simply is not true. The Bible *does* tell us what we need to know, and God will give us supernatural help to be *faithful to God's Word*.

Conclusion

Some people think children are not a blessing, and they are looking for a "return policy!" But children are, indeed, a wonderful blessing. Others think that children do not come with an instruction manual, but they do. We could call it a wisdom manual. They come with instructions from the one who created them and, for the Christian parent, they come with personal help from God. We can, with God's enabling grace and for his glory, faithfully honor God as we parent, even through the teen years. We can do it for *our* perfectly faithful Parent, whether even now the children are screaming at each other in the back seat of the car or thinking that David Peace killed Goliath!

Questions for Review

1. How does the goal of being faithful differ from typical goals of parents?

2. What do you think has been your main goal as a parent?

3. Do you have any questions about whether you are a born-again child of God, forgiven of your sins and looking to Jesus Christ alone as your Lord and Savior? What questions do you have? (See Appendix A and/or your study leader for further help.)

4. What would you say it means to be faithful as opposed to perfect? How does progressive growth (sanctification) fit into parenting?

5. What are the two basic responsibilities of the parent?

6. What are the two basic responsibilities of the child?

7. How is God using your children to sanctify you?

8. Who gets the credit for any faithfulness on your part and why?

Salvation and Sanctification of the Child

What could possibly be more important for Christian parents than their children being saved and living for the Lord? Is it possible for God to save children? Yes, certainly! But because of the very real danger of false professions of faith, this chapter is about presenting the gospel in its context to your child, and how to help the child who is really saved to grow and mature as a believer. Since the most vital thing Christian parents will do is teach the gospel truths to their children, let's begin with presenting the gospel.

The Gospel in Its Context

It is important to remember that there is not one gospel for adults and another for children. If God is opening children's eyes to the truth, they will truly comprehend all the basics of the gospel. You could think of it as adult-like content with child-like faith. While the children's version will be presented on a different level, all the elements of the gospel must be taught, understood, and embraced with a new heart for God before there is true conversion (Ezek. 36:26–27).

Children should be taught in their early years about God and reverencing him. They should be taught the doctrines particular to salvation. This is not the time to pressure them into any kind of decision to trust the Lord Jesus for their salvation. Instead, the pressure should be placed on the parents and church workers to be faithful to present the whole gospel at these early ages. Teach them diligently about God, man, sin, the law, and salvation "in accordance with the Scriptures" (1 Cor. 15:3).

In addition to living out your own relationship with Christ, begin slowly teaching your child little bits in story form from the Old Testament and the New Testament. Your goal is to instruct them about God so they will fear him through reverence and honor because "the fear of the LORD is the beginning of knowledge . . ." (Prov. 1:7). Remember to read the Scriptures to them, as this is the very Word of God. Then try to answer the questions they have. Reinforce during the week what the child has learned in church. However you do it, have some sort of systematic plan to teach them the stories while they are young (usually preschool and kindergarten), and then build on them as they are older and can understand more. Martha's daughter, Anna, is teaching her younger children Bible stories using a flannel graph to colorfully illustrate the stories. And, by the way, she is also teaching her two youngest girls to speak English, as they are from Ethiopia.

Another good way to teach them God's Word is through praise songs and hymns. Whatever avenues you use, their training should begin with a basic understanding about God.[1]

Understanding God

Children and teens need to understand that there is no one like God. He is unique, and it is amazing that he has told us what he is like. "To you it was shown, that you might know that the LORD is God; there is no other besides him" (Deut. 4:35). He is unique in that he is the *only* one great God made up of three distinct persons who dwell in unity (Gen. 1:26; John 10:30; Acts 5:3–4). The tri-unity of God or the *Trinity* is not easy to explain, but parents should study it and begin to teach the concept to their children. Since no example from everyday life is adequate to illustrate the Trinity, we suggest using Matthew 3:16–17, one of the clearest biblical examples of all three persons of the Trinity acting in concert, to help your children understand more about our triune God.[2]

1. There is a more in-depth gospel outline in Appendix A.
2. In this text, the Father speaks about the Son, and the Spirit descends on him to empower him for his earthly ministry. Heaven opening reminds us of Old Testament visions (e.g., Isa. 66:1; Ezek. 1:1), and the descent of the Spirit reminds us of God's promise that the Spirit would descend on his chosen Servant (Isa. 42:1). God's voice from heaven signifies the dawning of the messianic age (cf. Matt. 17:5; John 12:28), and reflects Isaiah 42:1, modified by Psalm 2:7 (cf. Matt. 12:18–21), thus linking Jesus with the Suffering Servant (cf. Isa. 42:1). "My Son" is an implicit reference to Jesus' title "Son of God," which is picked up three verses later (Matt. 4:3, 6), and Jesus' virgin birth (Matt. 1:23) suggests that he is the unique, eternal Son of God, a concept developed openly in the Gospel of John. The allusion to Psalm 2:7 identifies Jesus as the royal, messianic Son of David, the true Israel anticipated by the actual Israel. "These things are linked in the one utterance: at the very beginning of Jesus' public

God is also unique in that he has always existed. He existed in eternity past before he created the sun and moon and twenty-four-hour days. In other words, he was "before all time" (Jude 25). The prophet Isaiah quotes God as describing himself as " 'the One who is high and lifted up, *who inhabits eternity . . .*' " (Isa. 57:15, emphasis added).

God is not only eternal, but he is also our Creator. It explains a lot when children learn that "In the beginning, God created the heavens and the earth" (Gen. 1:1). "It is *he* who made us . . ." (Ps. 100:3). He is personally involved. See also Colossians 1:15–17.

> Thus says the LORD, your Redeemer, who formed you from the womb: "I am the LORD, who made all things; who alone stretched out the heavens, who spread out the earth by myself." (Isa. 44:24)

God, in his uniqueness, is also unfathomably *holy* and *just.* His holiness means that he is completely untainted by sin or inconsistency in who he is and in all his dealings. Unlike us, he is always righteous. His justice means that he will always be true to his standards and must separate himself from sin.

> "The Rock, his work is perfect, for all his ways are justice. A God of faithfulness and without iniquity, just and upright is he." (Deut. 32:4)

Most people would acknowledge that God is holy, but few recognize his justice. According to the Scriptures, two people

ministry, his Father presented him, in a veiled way, as the Davidic Messiah, the very Son of God, the representative of the people, and the Suffering Servant." Kenneth L. Barker and John R. Kohlenberger III, eds., *Zondervan NIV Bible Commentary* (Grand Rapids: Zondervan, 1994), 2:19.

got a sneak peek into God's throne room. One was Isaiah and the other was the apostle John. Both described seeing six-winged creatures flying around God's throne, and John recorded that they were saying, "Holy, holy, holy, is the Lord God Almighty . . ." (Rev. 4:8). Because God is holy, he has to punish sin. Therefore he is just. It is on the basis of God's justice that the apostle Paul preached:

"But now he commands all people everywhere to repent, because he has fixed a day on which he will judge the world in righteousness by a man whom he has appointed [the Lord Jesus Christ]; and of this he has given assurance to all by raising him from the dead." (Acts 17:30–31, explanation added)

Another piece of the puzzle to understand what God is like is that he is almighty and sovereign over his creation. This reminds us of a children's song that goes: "My God is so big (the children spread their arms out and open wide), so strong (they flex their muscles), and so mighty; there's nothing (shake their heads "no") my God cannot do (clap, clap)."[3] God *is* almighty and he *is* sovereign. "Sovereign" means he rules over his creation. One of the psalmists wrote, "For God is the King of all the earth; sing praises with a psalm! God reigns over the nations; God sits on his holy throne" (Ps. 47:7–8). God *is* our High King of Heaven.

Fortunately for us and our children, God is also merciful, compassionate, loving, and gracious! Jesus Christ, God in the flesh, came to earth and was "full of grace" (John

3. "My God Is So Big," in Sue Martin Gay, *Kids Classics Collection*, vol. 1 (Franklin, TN: Cedarmont Music, 1993).

1:14). Paul wrote a letter to the church at Corinth in which he praised God and said, "Blessed be the God and Father of our Lord Jesus Christ, *the Father of mercies* and God of all comfort . . ." (2 Cor. 1:3, emphasis added). Often one of the first Bible verses that a child is taught is the beloved John 3:16.

> For *God so loved the world*, that he gave his only son, that whoever believes in him should not perish but have eternal life. (John 3:16, emphasis added)

There is so much more that we could write about what God is like, but often even older children and teens do not know the very basics of the character of God. They must be taught. Otherwise, they will not have a reverential awe of him. We have seen some of what God is like, but what about man? What do the Scriptures teach about what man is like?

Who *Is* Man That Thou Art Mindful of Him?

Man was created sinless before the fall. He was to worship God, delight in him, reflect his glory, serve him, and proclaim his majesty. He was created to be loved, cared for, blessed by, taught by, satisfied by, and comforted by God, and to walk daily with him. Consider the following verses:

> "And now, Israel, what does the LORD your God require of you, but to fear the LORD your God, to walk in all his ways, to love him, to serve the LORD your God with all your heart and with all your soul." (Deut. 10:12)

20

You make known to me the path of life; in your presence there is fullness of joy; at your right hand are pleasures forevermore. (Ps. 16:11)

Whom have I in heaven but you? And there is nothing on earth that I desire besides you. My flesh and my heart may fail, but God is the strength of my heart and my portion forever. (Ps. 73:25–26)

Let them thank the LORD for his steadfast love, for his wondrous works to the children of men! For he satisfies the longing soul, and the hungry soul he fills with good things. (Ps. 107:8–9)

Therefore the LORD waits to be gracious to you, and therefore he exalts himself to show mercy to you. For the LORD is a God of justice; blessed are all those who wait for him. (Isa. 30:18)

Man was created to have a close relationship with his Creator, but when sin entered the picture, things changed drastically.

Our Sin Is Worse Than We Think

Sin, simply put, is breaking God's law. The apostle John explained that "sin *is* lawlessness" (1 John 3:4).[4] It began when Satan, who was created by God as an angel in heaven, rebelled against God. Satan was thrown out of heaven, and then in his craftiness deceived Eve into eating the forbidden fruit. If that

4. In answer to the question, "What is sin?" the Westminster Shorter Catechism explains, "Sin is any want of conformity unto, or transgression of, the law of God."

21

wasn't bad enough, she took the fruit to Adam, and although Adam knew full well the consequences of what he was doing, he ate it too. Sin is like an unrestrained disease: it spreads. "Therefore, just as sin came into the world through one man, and death through sin, and so death spread to all men because all sinned . . . " (Rom. 5:12). The Bible pictures sinful men as ". . . sheep [who] have gone astray; we have turned every one to his own way . . ." (Isa. 53:6).

Each man, woman, and child is responsible for choosing to sin and is thus separated from God, because God is holy. In Jeremiah 31:30 it is clear that "everyone shall die for his own sin." It is also clear from Scripture that our "iniquities have made a separation between [us] and [our] God" (Isa. 59:2, adaptation added). God cannot ignore the fact that he is holy, so his wrath is upon all the unsaved; and death, judgment, and hell are the results of our sin. The author of Hebrews explains, "It is appointed for man to die once, and after that comes judgment . . ." (Heb. 9:27). Sin affects every facet of our being—mind, will, emotions, and physical bodies. This is what theologians call *total depravity*. Because of God's restraining grace, total depravity does not mean that every man or child is as bad as he could possibly be. It does mean that every man does sin and is rightly deserving of God's wrath. Sadly, our sin is worse than we think it is; but conversely, God's grace is more wonderful than we can fathom (Rom. 5:20).

Grace, Grace, Wonderful Grace

Children need to be taught clearly that there is nothing *they* can do to take themselves out from under God's wrath.

No matter how good they are or how special they think they are, God's standard is complete holiness. No matter how hard they try, they cannot be perfect even if they grow up in a Christian home! No matter how sweet they are on the outside, they still have a depraved and selfish heart in need of God's grace. All children need a Savior to cleanse them from their sin and give them the perfect righteousness of God. That Savior can only be the Lord Jesus Christ, the perfect spotless Lamb, who came to earth to "give his life as a ransom for many" (Mark 10:45). Christ bore our sins in his body as he took the wrath and punishment that we deserve. The sin debt was fully paid for those who believe. "For Christ also suffered once for sins, the righteous for the unrighteous, that he might bring us to God, being put to death in the flesh but made alive in the spirit . . ." (1 Peter 3:18).

Only the God-man, who was sinless and did not deserve to die or be punished for sin, could satisfy the Father's wrath. Christ alone had the perfect righteousness that we need in order to be acceptable to God. Jesus' resurrection from the dead was the proof that he was who he said he was, and that he had accomplished by his death what he said he would accomplish. It was finished, and God's wrath appeased. Now God offers reconciliation by grace through faith in Christ alone. We can be ". . . brought near [to God] by the blood of Christ" (Eph. 2:13, explanation added).

If the only way we are brought near to God is through Christ, wise parents will be careful not to imply that their young children are already in a personal relationship with God, before they have responded to the gospel (2 Cor. 5:11–21). Neither will such a parent unsettle very young children with the harsh realities of their unsaved state before they can grasp the

23

gospel truths. Certainly even unsaved children can be taught to acknowledge, praise, and give thanks to God for who he is and for his common goodness to them (Ps. 150:6).[5] But this should not be confused with a reconciled relationship with God through Christ. For the most part, before they respond to the gospel, let your children be witnesses to *your* personal relationship through Christ, so they can see what God desires for *their* lives if and when they are saved.

At the time of salvation, God declares that those who believe are forgiven of all their sins (Col. 2:13). He also promises them the sure hope of heaven through the Lord Jesus Christ alone (1 Peter 1:3–4). "And there is salvation in no one else, for there is no other name under heaven given among men by which we must be saved" (Acts 4:12). True saving faith is a personal transfer of trust and reliance from oneself to Jesus Christ alone. This involves a godly sorrow and repentance that results in a turning from sin as well as a subsequent pursuit to love, trust, submit to, and follow the Lord Jesus Christ.

A real-life illustration of this change occurred when the Lord saved me (Stuart). I had been a rebellious teen who chose to go to a Christian boarding school in another state rather than stay at home with God-fearing parents. As soon as the Lord saved me, I became grieved over how I had offended God and mistreated my parents. So, I hitched a ride home (for part of the way in a garbage truck) and, much to my parents' surprise and joy, asked their forgiveness. You see,

5. That even the unsaved can give glory to God is taught in principle from Acts 12: 20–23 where King Herod (an unbeliever) was judged by God for not acknowledging God and giving him glory. About "common grace," J. I. Packer explains that God shows goodness to *all* (even the unsaved) in *some* ways (this is *common grace*), and to *some* (the saved), God shows goodness in *all* ways. This is *special grace*. J. I. Packer, *Knowing God* (Downers Grove, IL: InterVarsity Press, 1973), 147.

the evidence of salvation is not just a prayer prayed, but a new heart that turns *from* sin *to* Christ and continues to persevere by God's grace, "that those who live might no longer live for [the advantage of] themselves but for [the advantage of] him who for their sake died and was raised" (2 Cor. 5:15, explanation added).

At this point you may have thought of some questions. Consequently, we titled the next section . . .

But What About . . . ?

But what about the urgency of salvation? Although salvation is of the utmost importance, it is still wrong to pressure a young child for a "decision" for Jesus. If you do this you will likely encourage an uninformed or self-serving profession. We should call children to salvation when they have been taught what it means (Acts 16:31–32). Even then, their understanding and faith are a work of God.

> But to all who did receive him, who believed in his name, *he* gave the right to become children of God, *who were born*, not of blood nor of the will of the flesh nor of the will of man, but *of God.* (John 1:12–13, emphasis added)

> Blessed be the God and Father of our Lord Jesus Christ! According to his great mercy, *he* has caused us to be born again to a living hope through the resurrection of Jesus Christ from the dead, to an inheritance that is imperishable, undefiled, and unfading, kept in heaven for you, who by God's power are being guarded through faith for a salvation ready to be revealed in the last time. (1 Peter 1:3–5, emphasis added)

> No one can come to me unless the father who sent me draws
> him. And I will raise him up on the last day. (John 6:44)

We can rest assured that God will save his chosen in his time
and will not lose any of his elect (Eph. 1:4). The Lord Jesus
Christ expressed it this way, "All that the Father gives me will
come to me, and whoever comes to me I will *never* cast out"
(John 6:37, emphasis added). Instead of pressing your children for a commitment, teach and declare the gospel to them.
Christian parents are most certainly to be "ambassadors for
Christ, God making his appeal through [them]" (2 Cor. 5:20,
adaptation added).

But what about children who make a profession of faith
but do not live like it until later in life when they "rededi-
cate" their lives to the Lord Jesus? Often you hear testimonies that say, "I raised my hand in a Sunday school
class or walked an aisle when I was a child; if I had died I
would have gone to heaven. Then when I was a teenager,
I rededicated my life to the Lord and my life changed."
The problem with this thinking is that the Scriptures do
not teach anything like this experience (Titus 2:11–14).
What the person is describing about the rededication, if it
was turning from self and toward Christ, is what the Bible
describes as salvation.

> Therefore, if anyone is in Christ, he is a new creation. The old
> has passed away; behold, the new has come. (2 Cor. 5:17)

But what about a child who makes a clear profession of
faith, and his life does begin to change? Even if that is the case,
don't check off evangelism and go to discipleship only. Even

when discipling your child, it must be gospel-oriented. Early professions are suspect largely because of children's childish understanding but also because of their lack of being tested in their faith (1 Peter 1:6–7). Parents should not be convinced of their child's profession if the child is not, for the most part, persevering in faith and obedience to God's commands.

On the other hand, although questioning their salvation at times is understandable, be careful not to do so too quickly or frequently and frustrate them with your doubt. As the Lord Jesus taught in the parable of the wheat (representing believers) and the tares (representing unbelievers), the master (representing the Lord Jesus) will ultimately judge who is a Christian and who is not (Matt. 13:24–30). Often, it's not easy for us to judge fruit. There are snapshots of time in our own lives that would not look like we were saved either. Instead, look more at the habitual day-in and day-out lifestyle (the movie-strip film of one's life). Bottom line, we should encourage each spiritual step that a young child makes without assuming or assuring salvation (Matt. 7:17–23). Whether you think they are saved or not, keep teaching all the marvelous elements of the gospel to them. And by all means, do disciple them if they profess to be Christian!

But what about parenting an unsaved child? Well, the truth is that all Christian parents start out with an unsaved child. In fact, they may find themselves in the role of an evangelist their entire parenting years. Parents are still responsible to teach their children God's high and holy standards. Often unsaved children raised with Christian principles have better self-control and better character than an untrained, spoiled child. Thus, they get along better in the world, and they will likely be more attentive to your teaching. This would be God's common grace to the child and, don't forget, also to the parent!

But what about, "Train up a child in the way he should go; even when he is old he will not depart from it" (Prov. 22:6)? *Surely, you say, that is a guarantee to us from God!* Remember, Proverbs are not ironclad promises but general truths. For example, in general, "A gift in secret averts anger," but not always (Prov. 21:14). In general, "The glory of young men is their strength," but not all young men are strong (Prov. 20:29). And in general, "Train up a child in the way he should go; even when he is old he will not depart from it," but we know that some do depart. Proverbs 22:6 can be interpreted in many ways. Some think it refers to habits or to possessing a wise or foolish direction in life. Others think it refers to the way the child is inclined. What *is* sure is that it is a general truth, not an ironclad promise.

But what about, "But as for me and my house, we will serve the LORD" (Josh. 24:15)? Joshua's passionate speech was to the children of Israel to turn from idols to serving the Lord. He could no more decree that everyone in his household would be saved than he could decree that everyone in the nation of Israel would be saved. Joshua's declaration meant that inasmuch as he could influence those around him, he was going to serve God and teach those in his household to do the same.

But what about your thoughts that "it's not fair if God does not save my children especially after all that I have done." This struggle concerning the fairness of God is nothing new. Some in the church in Rome also questioned what God was doing. The apostle Paul had "great sorrow and unceasing anguish in [his] heart" because not all his Jewish kinsmen would be saved (Rom. 9:2). Paul's sorrow, however, was not the same as questioning God's goodness and his right to rule over his creation. Paul uses the example of God choosing Jacob to have God's special blessing instead of the custom of choosing Isaac's firstborn, Esau. He also uses the example of God's purposes in bringing Pharaoh to power. It was not to save him but to show God's power and that God's "name might be proclaimed in all the earth" (Rom. 9:17). Just as the potter has the right to mold the clay as he pleases, God has the right to have "mercy on whomever he wills, and he hardens whomever he wills" (Rom. 9:18). Since we do not know the end from the beginning or all that God considers, we all must humble ourselves before our all-wise, perfectly good, and sovereign Creator.

But what if you have additional questions or need further guidance in understanding and presenting the gospel truths to your child? We have made available more information in an extensive gospel outline in Appendix A. But for now let's turn to the question, "By God's grace I believe that my child *is* saved. Now what?"

The Sanctification of the Child

Certainly a child who is "in Christ *is* a new creation. The old has passed away; behold, the new has come" (2 Cor. 5:17, emphasis added). The child has a newness of life in his desires, and the vise grip that sin had over him has been rendered powerless (Rom. 6:4–6). The process of conforming to Christ's image has begun (Rom. 8:28–29). Now the child, by God's enabling grace, is to work at putting off the old self and putting on the new self which is being "created in the likeness of God

29

in true righteousness and holiness" (Eph. 4:22–24).[6] Ultimately, the sanctification process will be completed by God in heaven. So just what does the Bible teach about sanctification?

As we saw in chapter 1, sanctification means to be "set apart unto holiness."[7] It is both a God-given position and a process that God begins at the moment he saves a person, placing him "in [supernatural union with] Christ" (Rom. 6:11, explanation added). This God-given beginning aspect of sanctification is called *positional* sanctification. It is totally a work of God. Our actual change into holiness will be completed when Jesus returns for us or takes us to be with him through our death. Then we will be sinless "before the presence of his glory with great joy" (Jude 24). This aspect of sanctification is called *glorification*. It, too, is a work of God.

The Scriptures teach a third aspect of sanctification, *progressive*. This aspect differs from the other two as it is a work of God *and* a responsibility of man. The new believer is to yield himself to God and obey his commands. Man is to exercise what some Christians have called *holy sweat* while, at the same time, being

6. The Westminster Confession, Chapter XII, states:

I. They who are effectually called and regenerated, having a new heart and a new spirit created in them, are further sanctified, really and personally, through the virtue of Christ's death and resurrection, by His Word and Spirit dwelling in them; the dominion of the whole body of sin is destroyed, and the several lusts thereof are more and more weakened and mortified, and they more and more quickened and strengthened, in all saving graces, to the practice of true holiness, without which no man shall see the Lord.

II. This sanctification is throughout in the whole man, yet imperfect in this life; there abideth still some remnants of corruption in every part, whence ariseth a continual and irreconcilable war, the flesh lusting against the spirit, and the spirit against the flesh.

III. In which war, although the remaining corruption for a time may much prevail, yet, through the continual supply of strength from the sanctifying Spirit of Christ, the regenerate part doth overcome; and so the saints grow in grace, perfecting holiness in the fear of God.

7. Strong, *Words in the Greek Testament*, 1 (#37).

dependent on the Holy Spirit to energize his efforts for the glory of God. Paul said to "*train yourself* for godliness" (1 Tim. 4:7). So, parents, teach your saved children about sanctification so they can see God's grace as well as their responsibility.

One of the marvelous ways that God progresses a Christian child, as well as us, toward Christlikeness (not perfection but definite progress) is to test him. A test for a child may be a bully at school or an algebra test he must pass to make a final grade of C. Other tests may be learning to live peaceably with brothers and sisters or facing the death of a beloved pet. And, of course, even children may have to suffer extreme trials such as the death of a loved one. Trials and tests come in varying sizes, but with God's help, a Christian child can go through them by developing godly character. Thus, the child glorifies God even more.

> Count it all joy, my brothers, when you meet trials of various kinds, for you know that the *testing of your faith produces steadfastness.* And let steadfastness have its full effect, that you may be perfect and complete, lacking in nothing. . . . Blessed is the man who remains steadfast under trial, for when he has stood the test he will receive the crown of life, which God has promised to those who love him. (James 1:2–4, 12, emphasis added)

> Therefore, since we have been justified by faith, we have peace with God through our Lord Jesus Christ. Through him we have also obtained access by faith into this *grace in which we stand,* and we rejoice in hope of the glory of God. More than that, we rejoice in our sufferings, knowing that *suffering produces endurance, and endurance produces character, and character produces hope,* and hope does not put us to shame, because God's love has been poured into our hearts through the Holy Spirit who has been given to us. (Rom. 5:1–5, emphasis added)

Every child who is saved will begin the journey to become like Christ. Each trial in his life will take on new significance, because he does not have to go through it in vain. It has a good purpose in his life and in God's plan. This reminds us of what Joseph told his brothers after all the wicked things they did to him, "As for you, you meant evil against me, but God meant it for good..." (Gen. 50:20). God's purposes of glorifying himself and doing us good *will* be accomplished as a Christian, even a young one, is molded by God into the image of the Lord Jesus Christ. So be sure to help your child understand how trials and testing fit in this progressive part of his sanctification.

Take care that you do not seek to micromanage your children's faith or expect total sanctification *today* in their lives. You can't force them to grow, but you can lead them gently. For example, as they mature spiritually and in age, help *them* think through their choices and pursuits rather than just demand what you know to be wise and godly.

Children professing faith in Christ also need to be discipled and taught how the gospel applies to their daily lives. Some of the key areas to teach them are:

- Their position in Christ and how that is lived out.[8]
- The role of the Word of God in their lives and simple ways to have personal devotions.
- Prayer.

8. Because of the cross: Christ is with them; he has paid for and forgiven all their sins (past, present, and future); he does not treat them as their sins deserve; his perfect righteous life has been put to their account (making them acceptable to God); he is in them to empower them; he placed them in the family of God; he secured heaven for them to look forward to; he adopted them as his children to care for perfectly; he is coming back. He sacrificially gave and so should they; he forgave and so should they; he loved his enemies and so should they; he patiently endured and so can they.

- Personal worship/delight in God.
- Sanctification and the "Put Off"/"Put On" Dynamic (See Appendix B).[9]
- Renewing the mind (See Appendix D, Taking Thoughts Captive).
- How to discern idolatrous desires.[10]
- Spiritual warfare.[11]
- How to share their faith.
- Using their spiritual gifts and serving in the church.
- Basic Bible doctrines.[12]

Part of the discipleship process should involve the stewardship of all things given to the child by God: time, talents, money, possessions, etc. Young men who are maturing and teachable can be taught concerning masculinity, leadership, and decision-making from a biblical perspective, as well as the mandates of Ephesians 5:25–33 and Titus 2:6–8 and the godly characteristics of 1 Timothy 3 and Titus 1. Young women should be discipled through the mandates of Titus 2:3–5, Ephesians 5:22–24 and 33, and Proverbs 31:10–31. In addition to basic marriage preparation, growing Christian young people

9. The "put off"/"put on" dynamic is such an important New Testament concept that we have included more information about this in Appendix B: "Put Off"/ "Put On" Dynamic.

10. Discussion on these desires is found in chapter 7 of both Stuart Scott's book and Martha Peace's book. See Stuart Scott, *The Exemplary Husband* (Bemidji, MN: Focus Publishing, 2002); Martha Peace, *The Excellent Wife* (Bemidji, MN: Focus Publishing, 1999).

11. More on spiritual warfare from a biblical perspective is available from John MacArthur, *How to Meet the Enemy* (Wheaton, IL: Victor, 1992) and Richard Mayhue, *Unmasking Satan* (Grand Rapids: Kregel, 2000).

12. Some examples are Wayne A. Grudem, *Christian Beliefs* (Grand Rapids: Zondervan, 2005); Peter Jeffery, *Bitesize Theology* (Carlisle, PA: Evangelical Press, 2000); John MacArthur, *A Faith to Grow On* (Nashville: Tommy Nelson, 2000); Bruce A. Ware, *Big Truths for Young Hearts* (Wheaton, IL: Crossway, 2009).

should also be taught concerning the equal privilege of serving the Lord as a single person.

As your children evidence consistent faith and fruit, it will be time to teach them concerning their baptism (Matt. 28:19; Rom. 6:3–4), communion (1 Cor. 11:23–30), and church membership (Acts 2:42). Just like salvation, there needs to be a clear understanding and an embracing of what each means for them before your children participate. Don't rush into these very important commands of God for the true believer.

Conclusion

Parents teach their children many things to keep them safe. They often make endless sacrifices for their children's education. Most would die for their children if need be. Presenting a complete and clear gospel, in small segments at a time, is work for the parent, but there could not be any task more important. Only two things on earth last for eternity: one's soul and the Word of God. This is where the major investment must be made with your children.

As you seek to disciple your children in the things of the Lord, be sure to reiterate often that the Christian walk is about a relationship with an awesome God and Savior, rather than a list of do's and don'ts. We hope you will see a desire in your children to learn and grow, as well as a positive response to your efforts. But remember, you are ultimately seeking to be faithful to *your* Lord; the rest is up to the child, and ultimately God.

> "And these words that I command you today *shall be on your heart.* You shall teach them diligently to your children . . .

when you walk by the way . . . ." (Deut. 6:6–7, emphasis added)

Questions for Review

1. Although it is possible for children to be saved, what should parents do and not do in the early years?

2. What are some things that might be missing in an uninformed or false profession of faith?

3. What should you trust/keep in mind as you teach your children the truths of the whole gospel? What is it you cannot do?

4. Can the Christian parent claim God's promise to save children on the basis of Proverbs 22:6 or Joshua 24:15? Why or why not?

5. Whose responsibility is your children's progressive sanctification (daily change into Christlikeness)?

6. What are some ways you and your children could delight in the Lord Jesus Christ and his gospel on a daily basis?

7. What are some key things to exemplify and teach once your child has made a profession of faith and evidenced a change in heart and direction?

PART TWO

The Everyday Life

"Now this is the commandment, the statutes and the rules that the LORD your God commanded me to teach you, that you may do them in the land to which you are going over, to possess it, that you may fear the LORD your God, you and your son and your son's son, by keeping all his statutes and his commandments, which I command you, all the days of your life, and that your days may be long. Hear therefore, O Israel, and be careful to do them, that it may go well with you and that you may multiply greatly, as the LORD, the God of your fathers, has promised you, in a land flowing with milk and honey. 'Hear, O Israel: The LORD our God, the LORD is one. You shall love the LORD your God with all your heart and with all your soul and with all your might. And these words that I command you today shall be on your heart. You shall teach them diligently to your children, and shall talk of them when you sit in your house, and when you walk by the way, and when you lie down, and when you rise. You shall bind them as a sign on your hand, and they shall be as frontlets between your eyes. You shall write them on the doorposts of your house and on your gates.'" (Deut. 6:1–9)

3

The Infant

Twenty-five years ago, Martha met a young woman who was pregnant with her first child. They had several conversations about whether children were born with a sin nature. A few days after her precious baby was born, she called Martha to tell her that *her* newborn was pure and innocent, and that he certainly was not a sinner. They talked about what the Scriptures teach about the sin nature, but the issue was not settled in the young mother's mind. Six weeks later she called Martha back and said, "Do you remember what I said about my baby not being a sinner and being innocent? I changed my mind!"

Babies do come into the world as helpless and very dependent creatures. As a result, they certainly give the appearance of being innocent. Their heads are too big for their bodies, so they cannot hold their heads up or sit up until they are older and stronger. Just about all they can do is cry, eat, and cuddle.

They require nearly constant physical care, especially if they are fussy and colicky.

The time when babies are so tiny is very brief, as an amazing physical transition takes place from birth until he is twelve months old. Let's consider some general observations of typical children.

Developmental Milestones

Usually a newborn will cry, look around, and try to focus his eyes on his world. A six-week-old can focus his eyes, look at you, and smile back. By the time they are twelve months old, children can crawl, pull up, sit up, talk "baby talk" with great expression, and perhaps even say two or three words.

Newborns have a normal reaction to curl their fingers around an adult's finger. A twelve-month-old can pick up a very small crumb on the floor and put it in his mouth. Newborns apparently do not care who looks after them, whereas a twelve-month-old most certainly does care! Newborns, of course, cannot even turn themselves over, but a twelve-month-old can usually walk while holding onto the furniture.

When Martha's daughter, Anna, was expecting her first child, she asked her mom to come and help her when Tommy was born. Of course, that was no problem for Martha! Anna made it clear, "I want you to come take care of *me* and *I* want to take care of my baby." And so she did, with a little coaching from Grandmama. By the time Anna's twin girls were born two years later, as far as Anna was concerned, *anybody* was more than welcome to change the next diaper.

Like Anna, any inexperienced mother has to get over her awkwardness when bathing, dressing, and changing her newborn. By the time her baby is twelve months old, not only can the mother do these tasks easily but the baby can help by extending an arm or leg while being dressed or by lifting up his bottom during a diaper change.

We do not know what a newborn thinks, but we do know something of what a twelve-month-old thinks by the way he responds to simple requests such as being told "no." Most can say "uh-oh" when the dinner plate falls from the high chair tray. A twelve-month-old begins to understand the functional use of objects so that he can hold his cup to drink from it, use his spoon to feed himself, and hold a telephone receiver to hear his father's voice.

Infancy is a time when most parents have many questions. What do we do when . . . ? Is this normal? When will she sleep all night? A good pediatrician or even a commonsense grandmother can answer these and many more questions. But for the rest of this chapter, we want to consider what God tells us in his Word about these precious babies.

The Biblical View of the Infant

The Scriptures do not tell us much about babies. What we do learn, we glean from Scriptures that use the baby as an illustration of another point. For example, in the book of Lamentations, the Jewish people are warned of judgment to come because of their idolatry. Because of a small child's obvious vulnerability, the youngest ones would die first in the judgment.

> My eyes are spent with weeping . . . because infants and babies faint in the streets of the city. They cry to their mothers, "Where is bread and wine?" as they faint like a wounded man in the streets of the city, as their life is poured out on their mothers' bosom. (Lam. 2:11–12)

The point of Lamentations 2 is God's anger over the Jews' idolatry. The resulting catastrophic judgment is vividly pictured by the effect it would have on babies because of their vulnerability.

The first of three New Testament uses of babies as examples is found in Matthew 21:16.

> And they said to him, "Do you hear what these are saying?" And Jesus said to them, "Yes; have you never read, 'Out of the mouth of infants and nursing babies you have prepared praise'?"

In this passage a few days before the crucifixion, the Lord Jesus Christ is praised by young and old alike as he makes his "triumphal entry" to Jerusalem. Even though infants could not express the words, they bring him praise by virtue of being created by the Lord himself, and God has pity on them (see Col. 1:16 and Jonah 4:11).

Another New Testament illustration is one that the apostle Peter wrote to the Christians who were scattered throughout the Roman Empire. The purpose of his letter was to help them prepare for the horrific and not too distant persecution of Christians under the rule of Emperor Nero. Peter began his letter by giving the Christians great hope in their salvation, and then told them, "Therefore, preparing your minds for action, and being sober-minded, set your hope fully on the grace that will be brought to you at the revelation of Jesus Christ" (1 Peter 1:13). The way for them to "prepare" was through learning and obeying the "living and abiding word of God" (1 Peter 1:23). As a result, they were to be "like newborn infants, long[ing] for the pure spiritual milk, that by it you may grow up to salvation" (1 Peter 2:2, adaptation added). Almost anyone can relate to the picture of a baby longing for his mother's milk.

The third New Testament illustration is one the apostle Paul used in 1 Thessalonians. In this book Paul is defending himself against false accusations regarding his motives while preaching the gospel. God was Paul's witness that he "never came with words of flattery . . . nor with a pretext for greed . . . nor did [he] seek glory from people . . ." (1 Thess. 2:5–6, adaptation added). Instead, Paul's approach was gentle and tender, considering the Thessalonians as very dear to him.

> But we were gentle among you, like a nursing mother taking care of her own children. So, being affectionately desirous of you, we were ready to share with you not only the gospel of God but also our own selves, because you had become very dear to us. (1 Thess. 2:7–8)

Paul's illustration is of a gentle mother tenderly caring for her children. She thinks of her children as dear to her and for whom she has great affection. The nurturing love and care of a nursing mother is easily understood by mothers around the world.

Paul underscores the importance of the mother's tender care of her children in Titus 2, where the older women are instructed "to teach what is good, and so train the young women to love their husbands and children . . ." (Titus 2:3–4). This *philos* kind of love implies a tender, cherishing kind of affection. The mother should think of her child as someone *dear to her* and beloved.

I doubt there could ever be too many hugs, kisses, tender smiles, or expressions of joy from a mother or father toward their baby. Stuart's wife, Zondra, remembers that as long as she could fit both of her children, Christa and Marc, on her lap, she found time to rock and sing with them a tender song she wrote. It went like this, "Mommy loves Christa (or Marc) . . . Christa (or Marc) loves Mommy . . . they rocky rocky all the time . . . ," and on it would go about Daddy's love and Jesus' love, too. Zondra was tenderly loving and cherishing her babies. (And now Christa is tenderly loving and cherishing her own baby!)

Because we are to love and tenderly care for our babies, we must also love them enough to begin to "bring them up in the discipline and instruction of the Lord" (Eph. 6:4).

The Discipline of Infants

Just because babies cannot talk does not mean they cannot learn to listen and obey. They are always able to comprehend more than they can express verbally. Because of this, parents need to teach their babies "no" from the beginning.

Teach your baby to respond to your voice when you speak in a normal tone. As the baby reaches for something he is not supposed to have, calmly tell him "no" and move his little hand away from the object. If he persists, give him a tiny "spank" (explained later in this chapter).

Parents should also discipline their precious little infants for sinful attitudes. This is very rare, and if ever in doubt, *err on the side of mercy* and give your baby the benefit of the doubt. When a baby has a sinful attitude, it often is expressed in an angry cry accompanied by arching of his back while throwing his head back because he did not get his way. Calmly tell him, "No, I will not allow you to talk to me that way," and if he does not calm down right away, tell him, "No," and give him a little "spank."

Spank with your hand, and before you ever give your baby a little "pop," "pop" yourself on the back of your hand to make sure you are not using very much force. For babies, it usually is only one or two very light "pops" with your fingers to the back of their hands or on their fat little thighs. You only want to startle them a little, but if they persist in disobedience or a sinful attitude, you may have to "pop" their little hands a little bit harder.

Some people tell us never to spank our children with the hand as they will be afraid of your hand when you reach out to hug them or pick them up. We disagree, because a child who is afraid of a parent's hand or sudden movements of the hand is probably reacting to the parent's previous lashing out in anger and hitting in anger. Your hand is the safest way to know you are not overreacting and spanking too hard. *If you are sinfully angry, do not spank your child no matter what age they are*! You need to wait until you are under control before disciplining him. If you must wait to give a little "spank" to your baby until you are under control, do not spank him at all. An infant will not be able to make the connection between what he did thirty minutes ago and what is happening now.

When Martha's daughter, Anna, was six months old she discovered the joy of flipping over. She became good at it and was very fast, all the while giggling with glee. One day Anna began her "flipping over act" while Martha attempted to change her diaper. She turned Anna over and said, "No, you must stay still." Well, as Martha recalls, this went on about ten times in a row. It should not have taken so long, but Martha finally realized that Anna was not obeying. So she turned her back over from her latest "flip" and said, "No," and popped her fat little thigh. Anna never did it again! She cried, and so did Martha.

When dealing with a discipline issue for a baby, if you are unsure, always err on the side of mercy. Give him a little "pop" only if you are sure. Pray for wisdom from God. Many parents tell us that they do not discipline their baby because they think that "he is not old enough to understand." That is true, but discipline *and* instruction is how they *do* learn to obey and what "no" really means. Now let's turn to the issue of instruction in the Lord.

Instruction in the Lord

From the beginning of his little life, talk to your baby often. Smile and be expressive. No baby is too young to see the parents' joy when they talk about the Lord and his goodness.

A baby, especially as he approaches the age of one, is not too young to have books read to him. Simple books with wonderful color pictures will stimulate the brain as he matures in understanding. You can include simple books about God and our Lord Jesus. His attention span will be very short, perhaps only a minute or two, but make the time and effort.

Teach your baby about the blessing before meals. Some families hold hands, but whether that is your custom or not your baby can learn to be still and listen for a few seconds as you thank the Lord for your food.

Sing to your little one "psalms and hymns and spiritual songs" as you are "making melody to the Lord with all your heart" (Eph. 5:19). Often a mother's song of praise to the Lord will calm the heart of her cranky baby *and* the heart of a cranky mother! Certainly the mother's joy in the Lord will bring joy into the heart of any baby even if he is not old enough to comprehend the meaning. If you do not know simple Christian songs for children, ask the director of your children's ministry for suggestions or obtain a CD with children's songs about God. Teach yourself so that you can teach your child.

Give simple, clear instructions such as, "Obey Mommy and come here," while you have your arms outstretched to your baby. Another clear instruction is simply to say, "No," and at the same time move the baby's hand away from the electrical outlet. Soon your baby will learn to relate what you say with obedience. Be patient and kind while caring for your baby. Care for an infant is often pure *agape* love. It truly is a "labor of love" in the middle of the night or when you do not feel well. If you become overly sleep-deprived, tell someone that you need help.

It is easy when parents are tired to let their thoughts become sinful. The following chart contains examples of "middle of the night, sinful thoughts" compared with "*agape*, loving thoughts."

47

Middle of the Night, Sinful Thoughts	*Agape* Love Thoughts
1. "I can't take this any longer!"	1. "This is hard but God will give me the grace to endure as 'love . . . endures all things.'" (1 Cor. 13:7; 10:13)
2. "I wish he had never been born!"	2. "He is a blessing from God. One way he is a blessing is to help me grow as a Christian. I am glad he was born." (Ps. 127:3)
3. "Why is God doing this to me?"	3. "The Lord is testing me tonight and giving me a special opportunity to show love and to grow in God's grace." (James 1:2–3)
4. "This makes me so mad!"	4. "I chose to be mad. I am not forced by anyone else. Love is kind. I can show love to my baby by getting up and tenderly caring for her." (1 Cor. 13:4)
5. "I'm too tired to give any more."	5. "The faithful servant serves in the daytime or the night. I will pray and ask God to help me." (Luke 17:7–10; Heb. 4:16)

Over years of biblical counseling for parents and of being parents, Stuart and Martha have learned some tips to make life easier for the parent and the baby. These tips are not "thus saith the Lord," but they can be backed up with good-old biblical common sense.

Helpful Commonsense Tips

The first tip is to make certain you get enough sleep. Go to bed early instead of staying up late watching television or even catching up on chores. Even if they sleep all night, most babies wake up early raring to go. They are growing fast, and they are hungry. As tempting as it may be to finally have time for yourself late at night, go to bed and get as much sleep as you can. King Solomon wrote about this in Psalm 127:2: "It is in vain that you rise up early and go late to rest, eating the bread of anxious toil; for he gives to his beloved sleep." Discipline yourself to go to bed because you love your baby.

If possible, the mother should take a time to rest during the day for forty-five minutes or so in order that she will not be overwhelmed with weariness. If it is impossible for her to keep up with all her responsibilities (especially with a newborn), her husband needs to step up to the plate. It is the wife's responsibility to tell her husband when she needs help, since he cannot read her mind. She may also need outside help from the church family or her family. A mother should not wait until she is overwhelmed to ask for help. Anyone who has ever had a baby would understand.

Train your baby to go to sleep by himself in his crib instead of always waiting for him to fall asleep before you put him to bed. He may cry a little while at first. But be patient and wait. Then check on him to make sure he is all right. Everyone, including your baby, eventually will be much happier and get more rest.

Have a schedule but do not worship it. A schedule is only a helpful tool. It really helps to have a mother who stays home most of the time. That way she can put her baby down for a nap on a regular schedule. Have a plan for your schedule but "give thanks in all circumstances" if the Lord changes your plan (1 Thess. 5:18). For example, a wife receives a telephone call from her husband informing her that he has had a flat tire and needs her to pick him up. That wife has been providentially hindered by God.

Although it is good to have a schedule, do not sinfully judge other parents who are much more relaxed with their schedule and let their kids nap whenever and wherever. Some children think they live in a car! Even if they do, children can be well adjusted and brought up happy in the discipline and instruction of the Lord whether their schedule is rigid or not.

One word of caution for mothers who are breast-feeding. Sometimes your milk production decreases and your doctor will place you on a medication that will increase milk production. Because of the seriousness of possible side effects, you might want to consider your options.[1]

Conclusion

We have looked at the biblical view of the baby, and how children are not too young for parents to start laying a foundation of discipline and instruction in the Lord. They are also not too young to see their parents' joy in them and in the Lord. Babies are truly a gift from God:

> Behold, children are a heritage from the LORD, the fruit of the womb a reward. Like arrows in the hand of a warrior are the children of one's youth. Blessed is the man who fills his

---

1. A nursing mother is sometimes prescribed Reglan for milk production. Although it usually helps, it has several significant side effects. Before you take Reglan, you should consider that it can cause "restlessness, drowsiness, fatigue, sleeplessness, dizziness, anxiety, loss of muscle control, headache, muscle spasm, confusion, severe depression, convulsions, and hallucinations." And these are the more common side effects! Martha has counseled three young mothers on Reglan who began to have extreme anxiety accompanied by panic attacks. They had never had panic attacks previously. Therefore, carefully consider whether continuing to nurse is worth the risk. You have freedom in the Lord not to nurse your baby. It is far better not to breast-feed your baby than to possibly go berserk, develop some psychiatric disease, and be placed on additional mood-altering drugs. Then you would have to stop breast-feeding anyway.

quiver with them! He shall not be put to shame when he speaks with his enemies in the gate. (Ps. 127:3–5)

God blesses parents with a baby so they can love their child and marvel at God's creation. Babies are a gift to them from God, and they come with the added benefit of helping the parents grow in their walk with the Lord. A new baby is a testimony of God's goodness to them. Babies give parents a special opportunity to bow before the Lord and simply say:

Thank you so much for the wonder of this child
and help me to be the parent you want me to be with a
childlike trust in you and your good grace.

Questions for Review

1. Scriptures do not tell us much about infants. How do we learn about infants from the Bible? Give two examples.

2. According to the first two paragraphs under the heading "The Discipline of Infants," when and how should you begin to teach your baby to listen and obey?

3. Is it possible for an infant to have a sinful attitude? If so, what should you do?

4. For each category listed below, write out four specific examples of ways to bring your baby up in the instruction of the Lord.

   a. Smile and be expressive.

   b. Talk about the Lord with joy.

c. Read books and show pictures to them.

d. Teach them about the blessing before meals.

e. Sing to your baby.

f. Give simple, clear instructions.

5. What does it mean that "care for an infant is often pure *agape* love"?

6. Give three examples of wrong thoughts you have or might have had toward your children as babies.

7. Write out the correct thoughts for the three listed above. See Appendix D for help in doing this.

8. Re-read the "commonsense tips" at the end of this chapter. What others can you think of?

9. From the last paragraph in chapter 3, list all the ways that babies are a blessing. Can you think of others?

10. What is your prayer for your infant?

4

The Toddler

Often there is one person in a family who could be labeled the *weak link*. While the toddler is usually the cutest and funniest one, he or she can also be the biggest problem. Two- and three-year-olds are more likely to whine or scream at the slightest provocation. They want to talk and communicate, but often you cannot understand what they are saying. In addition, they are prone to major meltdowns that we call temper tantrums. And if that is not enough, they are the most likely to get into the cabinets and drink poison!

An example of how dangerous a toddler can act is the story of Martha's grandson, Matthew. One day Matthew's mom found him standing on a kitchen chair and stirring a large pot of boiling spaghetti. When his horrified mother pulled him away and asked, "Why did you do that?" with a smile, he said, "My help you!" Another day that week, he bit his baby brother, Noah, on the arm. When asked, "Why did you do that?" he exclaimed, "My taste him!" Toddlers are a great joy, but often they are a very *weak link.*

Developmental Milestones

Typically a toddler can roll a ball or color with a crayon (be sure to protect the walls). Usually they can listen to a story or music for five minutes or longer. Their speech is improving, and most can speak in complete sentences. They love to help their parents with chores but, of course, greatly slow down the parent. Most of them love to sing and dance to music and have a great deal of energy.

Their play is their work as they learn to stack blocks and turn pages in a book. It is always adorable when you ask a toddler, "How old are you?" and he really concentrates to hold up the two or three fingers. At this point in their growth, they begin to ask, "What's this?" and "Why?" It also occurs to them that they "want to do it themselves."

As their motor skills improve, toddlers can walk and climb; they can pull a chair over to a cabinet, climb up in it, and pull the dishes over on themselves. They can run laughing with glee and take off in full speed in the opposite direction from Mom or Dad who says, "Come here to me." The problem with their newfound joy is that they cannot discern when it really is cute and fun, or when they are running into the path of an oncoming car. So, they must be watched and protected. Often parents install safety latches on the cabinet doors or even some sort of alarm on the doors for the three-year-old who has learned to turn the knob and go outside.

The toddler's social graces leave a lot to be desired. Sharing with other toddlers is not their greatest character strength. Usually they get along better by playing *alongside* another toddler instead of *with* another toddler. They usually love to play outside and are typically following around someone such as a parent or an older brother or sister.

The Bible's Perspective of the Toddler

Like the infant, what we learn about the toddler in the Scriptures is not very much. The point of Old Testament stories is to show us what God was doing at that time, hence they are not a command from God on raising children. However, we do have some insights through the story of the young life of Samuel. Before his mother was even pregnant with Samuel, Hannah asked the Lord for a son and promised that if the Lord gave her one, she would dedicate him to the Lord.

Well, the Lord blessed Hannah and she bore a son. Even though Hannah loved Samuel dearly, she did not forget her promise. When Samuel was old enough to be weaned, she took him to Shiloh to live in the sanctuary and serve the Lord there.

The man Elkanah and all his house went up to offer to the LORD the yearly sacrifice and to pay his vow. But Hannah did not go up, for she said to her husband, "As soon as the child is weaned, I will bring him, so that he may appear in the presence of the LORD and dwell there forever." Elkanah her husband said to her, "Do what seems best to you; wait until you have weaned him; only, may the LORD establish his word." So the woman remained and nursed her son until she weaned him. And when she had weaned him, she took him up with her, along with a three-year-old bull, an ephah of flour, and a skin of wine, and she brought him to the house of the LORD at Shiloh. And the child was young. Then they slaughtered the bull, and they brought the child to Eli. (1 Sam. 1:21–25)

Samuel, like toddlers today, grew and changed rapidly until the time he was weaned. Even though the Lord blessed Hannah with other children, each year she would make Samuel a bigger robe and take it to him and visit with him. She must have been astonished year by year as she saw his physical growth and maturing from his childish ways. Samuel served the Lord through serving Eli, the high priest. Even though Samuel "did not yet know the LORD" in his early years, he grew up and God used him mightily as a prophet (1 Sam. 3:7). The discipline and instruction in Samuel's life began long before he was taken to live with Eli.

Discipline of a Toddler

A two- or three-year-old may be taught to obey the *first* time you give him an instruction. It would probably help your child if you practice with him how to respond.

Make sure you have your child's attention, speak in a normal tone of voice, and give a clear, age-appropriate instruction. Don't be too wordy or give more than one command at a time. It often helps if you bend down to the child's level and have eye contact. Do not confuse your child by giving an instruction and then adding, "OK?" The child will likely think he has an option and, of course, that is *not* OK.

If a mother tells her two-year-old, "Come here," her child will do one of five things: shake his head "no," run the other way laughing with glee, ignore her, come slowly with a pouting face, or come graciously. Anything other than coming graciously is either disobedience or a sinful attitude.

If the child disobeys or obeys with a sinful attitude, the parent has several choices: give up and try later, try to reason with the child, threaten to spank if the child does not respond by the time he or she counts to ten or snaps his or her fingers five times, repeat the instruction while yelling in anger, or simply go get the child and drag him to where he should be. Since none of those choices will achieve the righteous end that God and the parent desire, the biblical response most of the time is simply to spank the child.

Parents must realize that they have been providentially hindered by God and should stop whatever they were doing, if at all possible, and attend to the spanking. For example, a mother talking on the telephone to her friend would excuse herself from the call, hang up, discipline her child, and then call her friend back. Often the parent must sacrifice time, energy, and personal desires to obey the Lord and discipline the little one "while there is hope" (Prov. 19:18, NASB).

Calmly go to your child and spank him. Your motive should be love for your child and desire to obey the Lord. "Whoever spares the rod hates his son, but he who loves him is diligent to discipline him" (Prov. 13:24). Giving your child a little "pop" as he breezes by is not a spanking. That is only likely to provoke him to anger. For the toddler, we recommend beginning with three or four spanks to his little bottom. You want to spank him hard enough to cause a little sting but not hard enough to bruise him. Practice first on yourself (but not every time!).

Some children are very tender toward discipline, and it does not take much. On the other hand, some are hardened and perhaps physically bigger and stronger so they will require a little harder or more spanks.

The discipline should be sufficient so that the child is crying but not screaming in an angry rage. Years ago, Martha's daughter Anna was visiting with Stuart's family over a Thanksgiving holiday. Stuart and Zondra's son Marc asked Anna for some candy. Marc's mother said he could have it if he put the candy in his pocket and saved it until after dinner. Later on, but before dinner, Anna noticed that Marc's pants pocket was inside out. Anna asked, "Marc, did you lose your candy?" Marc, being an honest little fellow, said, "No, I ate it." Well, much could be said for not giving a little guy more temptation than he could bear, but as cute as it was with his telltale pocket hanging out, Marc had deliberately disobeyed.

His mom quietly took his hand, led him to the bathroom, and instructed him to wait until she returned. It was obvious to Marc that he was going to receive a spanking. Marc began to scream in anger, and his Grandpa commented, "Listen to that, his mother must be really beating him." Anna replied, "No, she is not even in there." Once the spanking was accomplished, Marc's cry became a softer, more repentant cry.

If Marc had continued to scream in anger, it is likely that the spanking was not long enough or hard enough. His mom would have needed to do it again. As the child grows older and bigger, you will have to adjust the gravity of the spanking in order not to leave him in a rage.

When you go to spank your child and you are angry, wait. Take time to pray and calm down so that you will not overreact. Never, ever slap or hit your child in the face or abdomen or choke or shake him. That is child abuse and assault. It is illegal, cruel, and wicked. Disciplining your child when you are out of control is sinful and will greatly provoke your child to anger. Instead of provoking your child, how should you lovingly spank him?

The Hebrew word for *rod* is *shebet*. It is a "stick or rod used for correction or punishment."[1] We are not going to dictate what kind of rod to use, but as the child grows bigger and stronger the parent, especially the mother, will usually need some sort of instrument for spanking. We do not recommend a switch from a tree because it could tear the child's skin. A belt is too long and the parent might accidentally spank the child in the wrong place. For the toddler, usually your hand is sufficient. Fathers need to be especially careful even when spanking with the hand as fathers are much stronger than mothers. If the child fights you when you go to spank him, do not begin until you have a good grip. This will prevent accidentally spanking him in the wrong place.

After the spanking, Mom or Dad should calmly talk with the child to make sure he knows what he did wrong and what he should have done instead. Also, teach the child to ask forgiveness. You will then grant forgiveness and give a hug, and that will be the end of the matter.

Some mothers or fathers have hurt feelings when the child disobeys. The parent might play it over and over in his or her mind, thinking, "If he loved me, he wouldn't do that!" That kind of thinking is unbiblical. Children are born as sinners with "folly in their hearts." It would not matter who the mother was, the child would sin. It is our pride that causes us to turn

---

1. James Strong, *The New Strong's Concise Dictionary of the Words in the Hebrew Bible* (Nashville: Thomas Nelson, 1995), 136 (#7626).

the child's disobedience into a personal hurt. Instead, the parent should deal matter-of-factly with the sin issue and then be finished with it.

What about the *Terrible Twos*?

Some think that being two years old has a rite of passage with a built-in excuse for temper meltdowns. Well, let's analyze this biblically. A two-year-old is not old enough or strong enough simply to take what he wants or to stop his parents from intervening. However, he *is* old enough and sinful enough to become angry at not having his way. Since he is not especially mature, he may cry, rage, scream, and/or flail in anger.

If the parent gives in, the child has learned that screaming in anger works—and works well. So he will likely do it again but scream louder and longer the next time. Some people think the best approach is to ignore it, and eventually the child will stop. While it is likely the child will get tired of screaming and eventually calm down, it is never good for a child to give full vent to his anger and to display such an incredible lack of self-control. God's remedy for this is to quickly go to the child, calmly tell him to stop, and then spank him, as, "Folly is bound up in the heart of a child, but the rod of discipline drives it far from him" (Prov. 22:15). Keep in mind that a two-year-old having a temper tantrum has the same heart as a sixteen-year-old screaming and swearing at his parents. The fool's heart is full of anger "for anger lodges in the bosom of fools" (Eccl. 7:9), and it is the rod of discipline that will drive out the folly. It is much better to begin at this stage of the child's life.

You may be thinking, "Spanking is so barbaric, but 'time out' is so civilized." Well, let's rethink this. Time out places a child who is raging in his heart into a seat. Then he plays over and over in his mind the circumstances that made him angry. Ultimately, the child will likely calm down, but it is not good for him to have all that time to brood in his heart.

What about distracting him to stop the tantrum? It is always good to be merciful and do what you can to make it easy for your child to obey. In James 3:17 Scripture tells us that God in his wisdom is "peaceable, gentle, open to reason, full of mercy and good fruits." Certainly we are to be like God. For example, give clear instruction and have your child on a reasonable schedule so he is getting enough rest. Feeding him helps, too. However, you are not doing your child any favors by manipulating him by way of distraction in order to avoid confrontation. Assume the best about your child, that he will graciously give in and obey whether he is tired or hungry or neither. If that does not happen, then obey God and discipline him or her. For the toddler, that almost always means a spanking.

Have a plan of what you will do in public (usually the grocery store) or if you are on the telephone or otherwise occupied. In any of these circumstances, when your child begins to whine, beg, cry, or create generalized mayhem, consider yourself to be *providentially hindered* by God. Regardless of the inconvenience to you, if at all possible stop what you are doing and discipline your child. If you are in public, this will be a judgment call. Ask the Lord for wisdom. It might be better to leave a cart half full of groceries and go somewhere private to spank your child than it would be to appease his sinful, angry demands.

Be calm and consistent and greatly honor the Lord by obeying him when you spank your child. At the same time, you will be demonstrating great love to your child as "he who loves him is diligent to discipline him" (Prov. 13:24). Parents who love their toddlers not only discipline them, but bring them up in the instruction of the Lord.

Biblical Instruction of a Toddler

> Fathers, do not provoke your children to anger, but bring them
> up in the discipline and instruction of the Lord. (Eph. 6:4)

Do you remember the Greek word for *instruction*? It is *nouthesia*, which means "place or set in the mind."[2] Children have to be taught and re-taught. It is especially important for a two- or three-year-old to be taught to obey for his own safety, your sanity, and God's glory.

In addition to teaching children to obey, you must teach them about God. There is a young mother, Tammy, whose son learned from observing his father how to lead a family devotional time. Benjamin conducted his own family devotional with his one-year-old sister, Ella. Ella listened wide-eyed as Benjamin pretended to read her a book about God. Finally Benjamin put the book down and said, "Well, there are no pictures of God in this book so I will just have to tell you what God is like. God is love."

Benjamin was trying to do what he had seen his dad do. His dad was obeying the Lord's command to instruct his children

---

2. James Strong, *The New Strong's Concise Dictionary of the Words in the Greek Testament* (Nashville: Thomas Nelson, 1995), 93 (#5219).

in the Lord. With young children, the teaching time should be simple and short—perhaps a ten-minute family worship time immediately after supper while the family is still at the table. For a toddler, the devotional should be concrete and clear. You could read part of one psalm and explain what that psalm teaches about God. For example, "Know that the LORD, he is God! It is he who made us . . ." (Ps. 100:3). From this, a child can learn that God created him or her and that God gave them to each other as a family. Therefore, isn't God powerful and good?

There are many good Christian books with wonderful pictures that are age appropriate for the toddler. Another way to instruct a toddler about God is to teach him praise songs that accurately reflect God's character and the Bible stories. Many a toddler has been entertained in the church nursery with an animated rendition of "Zacchaeus Was a Wee Little Man." Christian musical artists such as Judy Rogers have published and recorded quality children's songs. One that children especially like is "Go to the Ant, Oh Sluggard!"[3]

We learned earlier in this chapter about discipline of toddlers. Now we want to consider additional instruction for them to obey (Eph. 6:1). As we saw, *obey* is the Greek word *hupakouo*. It means to "listen with a view to obey."[4] As you teach your child to listen carefully and follow instructions, use biblical words such as *obey*. Say to your child, "I want you to listen to me carefully and cheerfully obey. Pick up these toys and put them in this basket."

3. Judy Rogers, *Go to the Ant* (Phillipsburg, NJ: Presbyterian and Reformed, 1989).
4. For a more thorough study on ways parents provoke their children to anger, we recommend Lou Priolo, *The Heart of Anger* (Amityville, NY: Calvary Press, 1997).

The first few times you instruct your children to obey, you will have to help them. For instance, kneel down and hold out your arms to them when you say, "Come here," or help them pick up the toys and place them in the basket.

The training and persevering principle is important here. The toddler likely will need to do the right thing accompanied by the right attitude over and over until he gets it right. The child who whines and then goes ballistic when an older sibling does not give him what he wants is not likely to stop complaining (whining) and exploding in a rage with one spanking and no instruction. After the spanking, say something like, "Son, you may not talk to your sister like that. 'Love is kind' and the Lord wants you to be kind when you speak and not angry. You may ask your sister for what you want, but you may not whine and become angry when the answer is 'no.'" It would help your child to have him practice the right response as you coach him.

For the child who seems to ignore you, make eye contact when you are giving an instruction that he is to obey. Even if he is incapable of understanding or following your instructions, it is important that he learn at least to graciously try.

Examples of Bringing Up a Toddler in Discipline and Instruction of the Lord

Since the greatest commandment in the Bible is to love God (by obeying him) and the second greatest commandment is to love others (by being patient, kind, etc.), it is extremely important that *parents* learn to think in practical terms of loving God and others. One way is for you to have a ready grasp in your own thinking of the *actions of love* in 1 Corinthians 13:4–7.

> Love is patient and kind; love does not envy or boast; it is not arrogant or rude. It does not insist on its own way; it is not irritable or resentful; it does not rejoice at wrongdoing, but rejoices with the truth. Love bears all things, believes all things, hopes all things, endures all things. (1 Cor. 13:4–7)

Be able to say these verses quickly from memory, in or out of order, and then teach your child the same thing. For example, "Love is patient. Sit here and wait patiently while I go get you something to eat." Or, "When you grabbed that toy from your sister's hand, you were being selfish and unkind. You were not showing love, as love 'does not insist on its own way' and 'love is . . . kind.'" (1 Cor. 13:4–5).

As you teach your child to think in terms of love for others, it is important to point it out when they *do* show love. For instance, "Thank you for waiting here quietly. You showed love to me because 'love is patient.'"

Something else you could do is teach your toddler to sit quietly and entertain himself. One word of caution, though, be reasonable. You might want to plan a time in your day to have your own quiet time with the Lord. Tell your toddler that you are going to read God's Word and pray, and he may play quietly beside you for five minutes. Give him something to play with and set an alarm clock or a kitchen timer. Explain that when the clock rings, he may talk to you if he wishes or make noise. If he does not make it to five minutes (and at first he probably won't), calmly stop reading and discipline him. If he begins to talk or make noise but realizes what he is doing and corrects himself by becoming quiet, simply go on reading.

After your child has successfully made it to five minutes for several days, add one minute to the time. As we mentioned earlier, be reasonable. Probably the maximum should be ten minutes for the two-year-old, fifteen minutes for the three-year-old, and twenty minutes for the almost four-year-old. Teaching him to show love by being patient would apply to many situations in his little life.

If you have your toddler with you in church, you might want to start gradually with a short time at the beginning of the service and then take him to the nursery. If you want to keep him with you the entire service, that is fine, but bring crayons or books for him to look at quietly without distracting others. Be prepared to take him out calmly and spank him if he does not obey. However, be sure to bring him back to the service after he is calm. Otherwise, the child may "consider the cost" and decide the spanking is worth it!

Toddlers need to see your joy in the Lord and your joy in them. Keep in mind that the ultimate focus should be on the goodness of God and not how special and worthy the child is. You might tell your child, "You are such a joy to me! The Lord gave you to us. Isn't God good?" (Ps. 100:5).

Even a two-year-old is not too young to begin to know the joy of Christian fellowship in your home and at church. Be hospitable to others in your home and participate in the fellowship of your church family. Let it be your joy and it will become your child's joy.

It is also important that your toddler see the delight in your face as you tell him about the Lord Jesus and about all of God's marvelous works. Point out that he or she is certainly one of those works as well as the animals, flowers, sun, moon, and stars, and don't forget his belly button! You can express to your child in words he can understand the same attitude that the psalmist had:

> O LORD, how manifold are your works! In wisdom have you made them all; the earth is full of your creatures. . . . May the glory of the LORD endure forever; may the LORD rejoice in his works . . . ." (Ps. 104:24, 31)

Even though a toddler is only two or three years old, it is not too early for him to begin to cheerfully do good deeds. Begin with letting him help with chores. Often this will slow you down, but do take a little time each day to teach him. You might want to begin by teaching him to pick up his toys. Have a basket or container in which it would be easy for him to place toys. Also, he is not too young to begin putting his dirty clothes in the clothes basket and trash in a trash can. Of course, that means he will need a clothes basket and a trash can. He will need a lot of personal guidance, but begin now teaching him to be neat and a good steward of things the Lord has given him.

Parents should express their delight in helping others. One example is a mother explaining to her three-year-old, "I'm cooking supper for Daddy and for you!" or "I'm baking a cake for Mrs. Smith because she is having out-of-town company."

Be gracious and thank your child when he does a good deed: "Thank you for doing that good deed. It really helped me, and God's Word, the Bible, says, 'And whatever you do, in word or deed, do everything in the name of the Lord Jesus, giving thanks to God the Father through him'" (Col. 3:17).

A toddler is not going to understand most of what that verse means, but *you* need to be thinking in biblical ways and, in turn, teach your child in simple words and phrases that he can begin to understand.

When you are around a two- or three-year old, it does not take long to realize he must learn to be gentle. Instruct him to be gentle in how he touches others. For example, he must pat his baby sister's head very gently instead of the typical *toddler death grip* as he hugs her. He also has to learn how to touch pets in a way that will not hurt them.

Work diligently and consistently when you instruct him, and discipline him when he does not have a gentle tone of voice. It is also important that *you* speak in a gentle and normal tone of voice. If he whines or has a harsh tone in his voice, calmly and gently tell him, "I am not going to permit you to talk to me like that. You are not honoring me. Say it again sweetly." Then coach him until he gets it right. Pray for wisdom to know whether to spank or not to spank. If you do spank, when the spanking is over and the child has calmed down, be sure to instruct him again concerning the original issue of the sinful tone.

We have seen several practical suggestions to bring your toddler up in the discipline and instruction of the Lord. Now we want to turn your attention to some additional helpful hints.

Helpful Commonsense Tips

1. Do not provoke a toddler by failing to allow sufficient time for naps and sleeping at night.

2. Allow yourself more time than you think necessary to get yourself and your toddler ready to go somewhere so that you will not be exasperated if providentially hindered. All experienced moms know that as soon as they try to leave home, one last diaper will be dirtied!

3. Be neat and organized with your home so that when you go to dress your child you know where to find both of his shoes!

4. Have a supply of over-the-counter medicines that your toddler may need in the middle of the night or during a snowstorm. Ask your pediatrician which ones to have. Have a thermometer available to take his temperature.

5. Toddler-proof your home by vacuuming often, and have child-proof locks on cabinets that contain cleaning supplies and medicines.

6. Lay out your children's clothes on Saturday night so there will not be panic on Sunday morning while getting ready for Sunday school. This would include matching socks and shoes.

7. Have some quick and easy meals on hand for days when your toddler is sick or you have had a difficult day.

Conclusion

Toddlers can be the greatest joy as well as the weakest link in the home. Taking care of them is hard work most days, but such an adventure. You will not always see the fruit of your labors of discipline and instruction immediately, but persevere by faith and trust in God. After all, you can faithfully obey the Lord and give him glory whether your child does or not.

Questions for Review

1. Why are toddlers so cute and why are they potentially dangerous?

2. What sort of safety precautions should you take?

3. From 1 Samuel 1, what do we learn about Samuel's early years? Later on in Samuel's life, how did God use him?

4. How many warnings should you give your toddler before you insist that he obey? What tone of voice should you use when you give an instruction?

5. List four practical ways you could practice teaching your toddler to obey.

6. What's wrong with this thought: "My child disobeyed me and it really hurts my feelings."

7. What's wrong with letting your toddler continue to scream in a tantrum? Why do we not recommend "time out" or simply distracting your child?

8. What are you going to do if your toddler has a temper tantrum in public (most likely the grocery store)?

9. What is the Greek word for *instruction*? What does it mean?

10. Write out two simple family devotionals that you could use with your toddler to teach him about God's character.

11. What are several children's praise songs that you could learn and then teach to your child?

12. What does the Greek word *hupotasso* mean?

13. List and memorize all the "love actions" in 1 Corinthians 13:4–7.

14. From the following scenarios, write out what you could say (in addition to possibly giving a spanking) to your child based on the "love actions" of 1 Corinthians 13:4–7:

   a. Your three-year-old pinches his puppy in anger.

   b. Your two-year-old is pouting even though he is outwardly obeying.

   c. Your toddler says in his loudest whiney voice, "I want a cookie!"

   d. Your three-year-old angrily pushes aside another toddler to grab a toy in the church nursery.

   e. Your three-year-old begins to sing loudly with glee after only two minutes playing during your quiet time. You had instructed him not to talk or sing for five minutes until the timer went off.

   f. One of the adults at church smiles and speaks to your child, and your child pulls away and turns from the adult and will not speak.

15. Read over the commonsense tips at the end of chapter 4. Think of any you could add.

16. What is your prayer for your toddlers?

5

The Preschooler

By the time a child reaches the age of four or five, there is usually considerable growth both physically and in maturity. Most preschoolers are much more trustworthy than a toddler. Even though parents must still take care to watch their children, preschoolers can usually play unsupervised for a time. They can also be much more helpful to others. One mother expressed it this way, "He has now become a real person!"

These little people can tell you what is happening in their lives. Some tell a condensed version, and you have to ask questions to really understand. One Sunday, four-year-old Joshua Regier told his Sunday school teacher, "My Daddy speaks Portuguese!" His surprised teacher replied, "He does?" "Yes," Joshua explained, "he's from Kansas." As the teacher later found out, the father *is* from Kansas but he grew up on the mission field in Brazil. Some children, like Joshua, tell a condensed version but others tell a long, drawn-out version of what happened, and you have to wait patiently until they are finished. If you try to get them to hurry up, they will just give more details.

This age group is delightful to teach if they have learned to be attentive and to listen. They should by now be coming to the point of gracious first-time obedience. How much freedom you give them will depend on how obedient they are (whether an adult is looking or not).

Developmental Milestones

Four- and five-year-olds can be taught to dial 911 in an emergency. They can also *answer* the phone. This can be good news or bad news! They can learn good manners, and instead of demanding their way, they can be taught to say, "Please" and "Thank you." They can learn to ask permission. One preschooler whose family stayed with the Peace family for one night on their way to a Florida vacation asked politely several times about different toys, "Mrs. Peace, may I borrow this?" The way he expressed himself reminded Martha of the verse that says, "and sweetness of speech increases persuasiveness" (Prov. 16:21).

Preschoolers can play age-appropriate games with others and listen to stories without grabbing the pages and turning ten at a time, and they proudly know all of their external body parts. A four-or five-year-old can usually blow his nose, which, by the way, is a happy day for his parents.

Four- or five-year-olds can usually dress themselves and brush their teeth with some help. They know the difference between big and little and know some colors and shapes. They can cut with scissors whether cutting paper or a sister's hair. They are becoming much more coordinated in kicking and throwing balls, buttoning their shirts, and tying their shoes. They can breeze past on a tricycle or a bicycle with training wheels.

A preschooler is growing and learning at a rapid rate. They truly are "real people now."

The Biblical View of the Preschooler

Four- and five-year-old children (and younger) can begin learning the Scriptures. We know of one church that teaches preschool children all the Bible stories, but they are taught in a more detailed way, *deeper* than the superficial way those stories are usually taught. The main emphasis concerns what God was doing. For example, in the story of Daniel and the Lions' Den, one of the conclusions points to God: "Praise God! Look what he has done. Angels do what God tells them. He is all powerful."

We know that Timothy, the apostle Paul's son in the faith, was taught by his mother and grandmother the truth of God's Word from childhood. Paul wrote about this to Timothy.

> But as for you [Timothy], continue in what you have learned and have firmly believed, knowing from whom you learned it and how from childhood you have been acquainted with the sacred writings, which are able to make you wise for salvation through faith in Christ Jesus. (2 Tim. 3:14–15, explanation added)

The sacred writings in Timothy's day were what we know of as the Old Testament. Now we have God's completed revelation to teach our children. We are to teach our children God's Word and pray that God will use what they learn as one of the means of grace that he uses to bring them to faith in Christ. The preschool years are informative years for children as they learn about God and to rightly fear him. Just like all children, the preschoolers' parents are to continue to "bring them up in the discipline and instruction of the Lord" (Eph. 6:4).

Discipline and Instruction in the Lord

If your four- or five-year-old does not graciously listen and obey, you must continue to work at training him. If he does not honor you with his tone of voice, with how he looks at you, or with his words, you should take the time to put your original instruction to him aside and coach him to restate the right words with the right tone. Then go back to the original instruction.

For example, you say to your preschooler, "It is time to put your toys in your toy box and come to supper." The child responds with a sigh and a whiney voice, "But Mom, I'll just have to get them back out again after supper!" At this point it is tempting for his mother to become angry and raise her voice and say, "Do as I say!" Instead of becoming angry, she should take time to instruct her child in a righteous response. She might calmly say, "Son, I am not going to let you talk to me like that (whining and sighing). Let's start over. I say to you, 'Put away your toys and come to supper.' What should you say and how should you say it?"

When you begin to train your child to speak graciously, you will need to give clear examples of his whiney voice as opposed to a gracious voice, of his sighing in disgust as opposed to looking at you respectfully, of his disrespectful words as opposed to his parent-honoring words. Think in terms of teaching him the right words, said in the right tone of voice, and with the right countenance. It would be wise on your part and likely would help your child if you do not wait until an incident arises, but teach your child specific examples of the right way to respond as opposed to the wrong way. Use examples that he can relate to and understand. Then when he responds in a disrespectful way, you can calmly remind him, "Don't forget that God's Word says, 'Honor your father and mother,' so how should you have said that in a way that would honor me?" (Eph. 6:2).

If your preschooler cooperates or even corrects himself in mid-sentence, you probably would not need to spank him. However, if what we call *the uglies* of his sinful, willful self continue to well up in his heart and come out of his mouth or show on his countenance, he probably will require a spanking. One word of caution: after the spanking, remember to continue to train your child by revisiting the original instruction. You might say, "Okay, son, let's start over. You are to put your toys in the toy box and come to supper. What should you say back to me?"

Ages four and five are fundamental years when there should be a lot of teaching, explaining what they are doing right as well as wrong, and correcting the wrong. Remember that children are taught in a lot of different ways, so be cautious about what they are exposed to. Even television commercials today contain sensual pictures and information that little ones (and adults for that matter!) should not be watching. Television, movies, books, and magazines are not in themselves sinful, but parents should be the filter for little eyes and hearts. Pray for wisdom and be aware of what your child is watching.

Preschool children can easily learn praise songs and have joy in singing. Even though almost all preschoolers are not yet Christians, they can learn a lot about God and our Lord Jesus Christ through hymns and praise songs. Martha has been teaching two of her grandchildren to play the piano. After the lessons, she has invited her youngest granddaughter, Kylee, to join the budding pianists in memorizing and learning to sing "Before the Throne of God Above."[1] Although she is barely four and cannot read, she joins in enthusiastically at church when everyone is singing that song. Her parents were greatly surprised.

There is a command in Scripture to be "filled with [controlled by] the Spirit, addressing one another in psalms and hymns and spiritual songs, singing and making melody to the Lord with all your heart" (Eph. 5:18–19, explanation added). Even if you cannot carry a tune, you can play wonderful praise songs and hymns on your radio or CD player in your home and teach them to your children. One word of reminder: we teach our children these things so they can learn about God and have a proper worldview and see our joy in the Lord, not because we think they are already or automatically Christians.

Continue to work on teaching your children to obey. The basic meaning for "obey" is to *listen*. Therefore, work at instructing them about the Lord by reading or telling Bible stories and then asking questions to see how well they listened and comprehended. An example from the story of Daniel and the Lions' Den (Dan. 6) could include questions such as "What

1. Words by Charitie L. Bancroft (1841–92) and music by Vicki Cook, *Worship Together 4.0* (Brentwood, TN: Worship Together, 2001).

happened to Daniel?" "Why was he put in the lions' den?" "Do you think he was scared?" "Why did the king stay awake all night?" "What was the king's name?" "How did God keep the lions from killing Daniel?" Teaching your child this way will help him learn to listen and to think. It will make it easier for him to pay attention to his Sunday school teacher and, in the future, his regular school teacher.

These early years are informative for the children. They learn about God's holiness and that their sin separates them from God. Like adults, they will tend to sin the same sins over and over. Use this, as Pastor Tedd Tripp says, as a "springboard for the gospel."[2]

Suppose your child angrily snatches a toy away from her little brother for the third time (that you know of) that day. In addition to appropriate discipline, you might want to instruct your child in her need for the Lord. For instance, "Your anger and bullying your brother keeps happening because you need the Lord to save you and to help you. God made us so he requires us to do what is right. He is holy and always does what is right. He never, ever sins, but you and I do. The only way we can have a right relationship with God, and receive help from him to do the right thing, is to be saved. When God saves us, he forgives us and gives us a new heart to believe him and to turn away from our sin. Let me explain how God decided to save some people like you and me: God the Father sent the Son, the Lord Jesus Christ, to earth. He lived the perfect life that we are supposed to live but don't. Then at the end of his life, he died on the cross. While on the cross, he bore our sins in his body. That means he took the punishment in our place

2. Tedd Tripp, *Shepherding a Child's Heart* (Wapwallopen, PA: Shepherd Press, 1995), 22.

that we deserve for our sins. He did that because he loves us, not because we can be good enough to deserve it. Then he arose from the dead and lives to intercede for believers when they sin. The Bible tells us, "Believe in the Lord Jesus, and you will be saved" (Acts 16:31).

As your child grows older, you can give him more information and many more Bible verses. Remember that you are being used by God to plant seeds in your child's mind. You do not have to tell him every single thing about the gospel every time. Although it is very tempting to try to nail down the child's commitment by leading him in a rote prayer, we do not recommend it. As we said in an earlier chapter, many children pray salvation prayers because they want to please their parents or they want to avoid hell. These are wrong motives, and children who have them do not understand their need for Christ. Does God save children? Is it all right if your child says he wants to pray for God to save him? Certainly, but only time will tell if his profession of faith is genuine. We do not want to give any child a false assurance. Instead, we want to be faithful to "bring them up in the discipline and instruction of the Lord" (Eph. 6:4).

Helpful Commonsense Tips

- Help your preschooler complete his daily "duties" by teaching him to remember them on his fingers. For example, finger number one is make my bed, finger number two is brush my teeth, finger number three is get dressed, etc. When all five duties are done, then come to Mommy and give her a "high five."

- Work *with* your children to do chores until they are capable, then work *beside* them until they can be trusted to work alone, then *check behind* them (at least for a while) to see whether they did a good job. If your child did not, call him back to do it over.
- Be sure your children have adequate rest. If they do not take a nap, simply give them a rest period some time in the afternoon. Perhaps they could look at books quietly.
- Practice social skills with them such as looking at the person who is talking to them and speaking loud enough so the other person can hear. If saying "please" and "thank you" is not already a habit for your children, work at reminding them.
- Age-appropriate games and puzzles are fun for the four- or five-year-old, and helpful to prepare them for school.
- Preschoolers need lots of play time and exercise. Don't let their day be consumed with cartoons and movies.
- Be discerning about the cartoons and movies you let your child watch.

Conclusion

The preschool years are usually delightful for this "real little person" and his parents. Every day is an adventure as he discovers bugs and worms and learns to count and color. Or it is an adventure for her as she helps her mother mix up the cookie dough and carefully tucks her baby doll in bed for the night. Every day is also an adventure in God's grace for their parents as they learn to faithfully share the Lord Jesus Christ with their child.

Questions for Review

1. According to the third paragraph in chapter 5,, how would you determine how much freedom to give a preschooler?

2. The Old Testament stories' main emphasis is on what God is doing. What could you say to your preschooler is one of the main points in the following stories:

   a. Daniel and the lions' den

   b. Joshua and the Battle of Jericho

   c. Joseph's coat of many colors and his brothers' jealousy

   d. The first rainbow

   e. The tower of Babel

3. When you are instructing your preschool child to graciously respond, what three areas should you concentrate on? See the third paragraph under "discipline and instruction of the Lord."

4. Why do we teach our children about God?

5. Write out at least four examples of questions you could ask your preschooler (so he can learn to be attentive) after he has heard the following Bible story:

   a. The creation account

   b. Adam and Eve

   c. Noah and the flood

   d. Joseph and the famine

6. When your child keeps repeating sins, write out what you could say to him because he needs the Lord. Hint: write out a simple gospel presentation that you could tell your preschooler. Be sure to use Scripture to back up your main points.

7. Read over the commonsense tips and see how many you can add.

8. What is your prayer for your preschooler?

6

The School-age Child

School-age children are six to twelve years old. In general, they are industrious and want to please their parents. One of Martha's grandchildren, Carter, is six. Recently he built himself a table with scrap wood gathered from his dad's shop. Although the hammer seemed almost as big as he, Carter patiently hammered many nails into the top four corners of the little table to secure the legs. He proudly shows it off to anyone who will look at it. His carpenter skills will only increase as he grows older.

Cameron, Carter's older brother, is strong and loves to help his dad work in the shop. Often you can see him handing David various tools, screws, or nails. He is David's number one helper. Another of David and Jaimee's boys is Caleb, who is twelve. Caleb is tall, as he has recently shot up like a bean stalk. He loves to study and has a special interest in marine biology. His entire room has a nautical theme, complete with three fish tanks. Caleb can tell you the common name, the scientific name, and the proper care of all his fish.

School-age children have the ability to grasp concepts and think abstractly. They are learning to care for themselves and, as they grow older, they can acquire many new skills such as cooking, playing the piano, and washing their own clothes. They are very busy with school work and other activities. They have a lot of energy but still require a good night's sleep. We know a lot about children ages six to twelve just through being parents and commonsense observations, but what about the child spiritually?

Biblical View of the School-age Child

Scripture tells us that even a child can be wise. In Ecclesiastes 4:13, King Solomon compares the wisdom of some children to the foolishness of some kings. "Better was a poor and wise youth than an old and foolish king who no longer knew how to take advice." We want our children to be wise, so we must teach them Bible doctrine.

Doctrine is simply what the Bible teaches about a particular subject. For instance, some doctrines were covered in chapter 2: God the Trinity, the atoning work of the Lord Jesus Christ on the cross, man, and sin. It is clear from both the Old and New Testaments that God commands parents to instruct their children in Bible doctrine.

"Hear, O Israel: The LORD our God, the LORD is one. You shall love the LORD your God with all your heart and with all your soul and with all your might. And these words that I command you today shall be on your heart. You shall teach them diligently to your children, and shall talk to them when you sit in your house, and when you walk by the way, and when you lie down, and when you rise. You shall bind them as a sign on your hand, and they shall be as frontlets between your eyes. You shall write them on the doorposts of your house and on your gates." (Deut. 6:4–9)

If you are going to teach your children about God, you must first know these things yourself. You cannot teach or explain something you do not know or about which you only have a vague idea. Therefore, work hard to study basic Bible doctrine.

Ask Yourself These Questions[1]

- How would I explain to my school-age child what God is like?
- How many of God's attributes can I name?
- What is at least one main Scripture I could quote or easily find in the Bible to show each of God's attributes?
- Could I clearly give an accurate gospel presentation?
- What would I say that would be appropriate for my child's level of understanding?
- What would I tell my child about other religions?
- Which Scriptures would you show your child so he could know the Bible is true?

1. See the following resources: John MacArthur, *A Faith to Grow On* (Nashville: Tommy Nelson, 2000); Bruce A. Ware, *Big Truths for Young Hearts* (Wheaton, IL: Crossway, 2009).

- How would you give your child hope in the midst of a difficult situation?
- How would you explain to your child that he is to "overcome evil with good" when someone is bullying him? Do you know where that Scripture is found?

These questions are just a sampling of what the ordinary Christian should know. These precious truths are for all Christians, not just the pastor! If you cannot answer these questions easily through using Scripture, get to work. Study them for yourself, write out your answers and place them in your Bible, review them regularly, and meditate on and memorize the Scriptures. Then, they will always be on the tip of your tongue.

Discipline and Instruction in the Lord

Most school-age children soak up knowledge like a sponge soaks up water. I, Stuart, can remember my mom (a retired elementary school teacher and principal) saying she loved teaching the school-age child for this reason. Often as a result of growing up in a Christian home and being exposed to the gospel, these children will make a profession of faith. As we have said in previous chapters, your child may or may not really be a Christian. Many at this age profess Christ and seemingly show fruit such as expressing joy in talking about the Lord.

Only God can really know whether your child is acting out of true godly character or simply because of good habits learned from you. So from time to time you might want to say to your child who believes himself to be saved (and he really might be), "If the Lord has truly saved you (and he might have), it greatly honors the Lord and it will be your joy when you do what pleases him. Time will tell, but in the meantime here are some of the areas the Lord wants you to work on . . . ."

Good Deeds

One area is to teach your child to do good deeds for others. Scripture says, "Even a child makes himself known by his acts, by whether his conduct is pure and upright" (Prov. 20:11). At Christmastime, the Scotts made a special effort to instill in their children that it is "more blessed to give than to receive." Even when Christa and Marc were young, they developed a love of giving gifts to others. Their joy as well as the gift brought the recipient a lot of joy. In this, they were known by their parents for their good deeds.

One homeschooling mom sent her fifth-grade daughter with a family friend each week to visit the friend's elderly relative in a nursing home. Robyn was a great joy both to the person visited and to the adult visiting with her. Robyn was not a Christian at that time, but she was learning to do good deeds for others and to be a servant.

Praising God

Another area to teach your child is to praise the Lord. All children, whether Christians or not, should praise and thank God. He deserves it. Psalm 148 tells all of God's creation to praise him, and that includes powerful kings or lowly children.

> Praise the LORD! Praise the LORD from the heavens; praise him in the heights! . . . Praise the LORD from the earth, you great sea creatures and all deeps, fire and hail, snow and mist, stormy wind fulfilling his word! Mountains and all hills, fruit trees and all cedars! Beasts and all livestock, creeping things and flying birds! Kings of the earth and all peoples, princes and all rulers of the earth! Young men and maidens together, old men and children! Let them praise the name of the LORD, for his name alone is exalted, his majesty is above earth and heaven. (Ps. 148:1, 7–13)

Children can praise God by their simple prayers as well as by singing hymns and praise songs. Some churches have a "hymn of the month." The music minister selects the hymn and then provides sheets with the words. Many of the parents help their children memorize the words. It becomes obvious to everyone on Sundays what that month's hymn is when the children join with the adults in praising God with their singing.

Even if your church does not provide a "hymn of the month" program, you can do this for your children. Perhaps your music minister would give you a list of the hymns or praise songs that will be sung the following month in church. Even if you have no musical ability, you could choose one of the songs and help your children memorize words. You can also provide children's praise song CDs for them to hear at home or in the car.

Music is a primary way for us to praise and thank God, but simply being grateful day in and day out is another way. Parents should think in grateful terms and influence their children to do the same. For instance, speak as if you mean it when saying the blessing before a meal, or have the same kind of attitude about the Lord's death on the cross that the apostle Paul had when he wrote, "Thanks be to God for his inexpressible gift!" (2 Cor. 9:15).

Good Character Habits

All parents should teach and work at developing in their children good character habits such as wisdom, hard work, cheerfulness, and kindness. Children trained in these ways are more likely to get along with others as adults than children who are not. Then if the Lord saves them, they truly will be manifesting godly character and not simply good habits.

Friendships

Most school-age children develop friendships with other children outside their families. You should get to know their friends so you may be discerning about their character as well as your children's. Because "bad company ruins good morals" (1 Cor. 15:33), you should make an effort to be around enough to protect your child if necessary. School-age children should not be left to their own devices for hours on end. Ask God for wisdom, and check on your children from time to time. Do be discerning about the character of your children's playmates.

As a word of caution, many parents become defensive if another parent comes to them with a concern about their child. Instead, be humble and consider the possibility that your child may have done what that parent reported. Do hear your child's side of the story and, if the stories conflict, you may need to talk with other witnesses. However, keep in the back of your mind that many parents have unwittingly made fools of themselves by vehemently defending their children only to find out later that their child really was the one at fault!

Bible Knowledge

School-age children learn many basic things in school such as science, math, and grammar. These provide a foundation for advanced study in high school and perhaps college. These are the years to go beyond the basic Bible stories they should have already learned and teach them how to find things in the Bible. This does not have to be all drudgery. You can make it fun with "sword drills" as in Sunday school with children competing to see who can locate a verse first. Early in their school years, they should memorize and recite the names of the books of the Bible.

Another discipline to teach your children is Scripture memory. This could be a family project that includes Mom and Dad! Go over a selected Scripture passage aloud at a convenient time for the family. Often families are together at supper, and work on the verse/s of the week or month should not take more than five minutes or so. This Scripture "stored up . . . in [their] heart[s]" (Ps. 119:11, explanation added) can be used by the Holy Spirit for salvation. The memory verse can also influence the unsaved child's conscience to do what is right and, by God's grace, will enable the saved child to give God great glory. The Christian child could sincerely say to God with the psalmist, "Your testimonies are my heritage forever, for they are the joy of my heart" (Ps. 119:111).

School-age children, especially as they grow older, should be taught basic skills of how to study the Scriptures. For example, teach them a clear understanding of the *big picture* of chronological history from creation until the Lord comes back. This will enable them to understand how and where the children's Bible stories fit into the history of the world, how the prophets point toward Christ, and how Christians have the hope that when Christ comes back "that at the name of Jesus every knee should bow, in heaven and on earth and under the earth, and every tongue confess that Jesus Christ is Lord, to the glory of God the Father" (Phil. 2:10–11).

Teach the older school-age children how to use a Bible concordance. A concordance is a book or a computer program that lists every word in the Bible and tells you where it is located. For example, if the child wanted to learn what the Bible teaches about anger, he could look up *anger* in the concordance and find a list of every verse in the Bible that contains the word *anger*. One word of caution, to prevent undue confusion, be sure to obtain a concordance that is the same translation as your child's Bible.

Biblical Communication

In addition to basic Bible study skills, teach your children how to interact with others in a biblical way. Parents should expect a two-year-old to play happily beside another two-year-old, but they should expect a school-age child to communicate biblically, solve conflicts biblically, and grant and receive forgiveness.

Learning to communicate biblically is a lifelong process for all of us, even if we are Christians and love the Lord! Communicating biblically means "speaking the truth in love" (Eph. 4:15) and responding with a patient and kind tone of voice because "Love *is* patient and kind" (1 Cor. 13:4, emphasis added). Biblical communication means to be "quick to hear, slow to speak, slow to anger" (James 1:19). It also means putting off corrupt speech and putting in its place edifying speech.

> Let no corrupting talk come out of your mouths, but only such as is good for building up, as fits the occasion, that it may give grace to those who hear. (Eph. 4:29)

Children will need to be taught and coached at times to rethink and restate what they *should* have said and *how* they should have said it. The same holds true for their parents. There will likely be many times that you need to say to your child, "This sinful speech and ugly tone of voice keeps happening. This shows how much you need the Lord." Then follow up with the gospel.

In addition to teaching your child to communicate biblically, you need to instruct him on how to solve conflict biblically. The way to solve a conflict depends on the situation. Conflicts can occur over righteousness issues, because of selfishness, or simply from being different. An example of a righteousness conflict would be if another child tries to cheat by asking to look at your child's paper during a test.

You can prepare your child for such an event. Instruct him that if this ever happens, he should say something like, "No, you may not cheat off my paper, and what you are asking is not right." If the other child persists, then your child needs to know that it *is* biblical to involve an adult. Explain that the child's motive in involving an adult should be to help the other child do what is right. Galatians 6:1 instructs us to "restore [the erring brother] in a spirit of gentleness." Without the right motive, the child would be acting as a tattletale who delights in getting the other person in trouble.

It is a fact of life that people are different. If a conflict occurs over an issue of being different, teach your child that it is all right if others have different likes or dislikes. These are areas in which we have *freedom in the Lord*. It's okay if one child prefers a jungle theme in his room and another wants a nautical theme. One of the character qualities of a godly person during conflict is to forbear with others who have different likes and dislikes (Eph. 4:1–3). That means putting up with differences in others. Parents, as you teach your children about differentness, be sure to understand it yourself. Although you have full authority from God to override your child's decorating tastes, at least take into account that what you think is ugly may be incredibly beautiful in the child's eyes. So, model forbearance as much as you can!

The most common cause of conflict is selfishness; children are renowned for behaving selfishly. Parents should teach them to follow the selfless, "thinking of others" kind of love that Jesus had for them (Phil. 2:3–8). For example, they are not born being glad it is the other child's birthday and not theirs. Sharing is a foreign concept as is *being glad for the other person*. Explain to your child that the biblical antidote to selfishness is love and love "does not insist on its own way" (1 Cor. 13:5). In addition, teach your child to think in terms of being glad for the other person when the other child has better grades, wins the monopoly game, or plays the piano better than he does.

In addition to resolving conflict biblically, children must learn to grant and receive forgiveness.

> Let all bitterness and wrath and anger and clamor and slander be put away from you, along with all malice. [Instead,] be kind to one another, tenderhearted, forgiving one another, as God in Christ forgave you. (Eph. 4:31–32, adaptation added)

All children will be sinned against from time to time, whether it is by their friend, their sibling, or even their parent. Teach them what to do when someone comes to them and says, "Will you forgive me?" The answer is, "Yes." Help them realize that we all sin and are in need of forgiveness whether we have sinned against God or another person. A person who refuses to forgive is cruel, hard-hearted, and proud, like the person who punishes others by not speaking to them. They are characterized in Scripture as people who are wicked and will not be forgiven by God (Matt. 18:21–35). The Lord Jesus' instructions are clear:

> "Pay attention to yourselves! If your brother sins, rebuke him, and if he repents, forgive him, and if he sins against you seven times in the day, and turns to you seven times, saying 'I repent,' you must forgive him." (Luke 17:3–4)

If your child has done something for which he should ask forgiveness, teach him to do this as quickly as possible. The Lord expressed the urgency when he used the example of someone going to church to leave an offering and, at that time, remembering that a brother has something against him:

"So if you are offering your gift at the altar and there remember that your brother has something against you, leave your gift there before the altar and go. First be reconciled to your brother, and then come and offer your gift." (Matt. 5:23–24)

Often children are too proud to ask forgiveness. Make sure that it is not because you as the parent are too proud to ask forgiveness! If your child is stubborn and refuses to ask forgiveness, then some sort of appropriate biblical discipline is in order. For the younger school-age child, it would usually be a spanking. For the older school-age child, it might be some sort of restriction or sending to a *think room* to consider what he has done wrong and what he should be doing about it. For children of all ages, this is a God-given opportunity for the parents to be "ambassadors for Christ, God making his appeal through us. We implore you on behalf of Christ, be reconciled to God" (2 Cor. 5:20).

Seeking and granting forgiveness are at the heart of the Christian faith. Another important principle from Scripture is learning to obey whether you feel like it or not. Teach your school-age child that the supreme example of obedience is the Lord Jesus when he faced arrest and the cross. In spite of his soul being "very sorrowful, even to death" and praying, "My Father, if it be possible, let this cup pass from me: nevertheless, not as I will, but as you will," Jesus obeyed and carried out the will of his Father (Matt. 26:38–39). Children, just like adults, can be wrongly controlled by their emotions. They must be taught to do the right thing whether they feel like it or not. For the unsaved child, his rewards will be that he has pleased his parents and he will get in a lot less trouble. For the saved child, he will glorify his Father in heaven (and also get in a lot less trouble!).

Helpful Commonsense Tips

- Have reasonable control over your child's schedule and don't let outside activities such as sports rule your life.
- Use chores and/or pets to instill the character qualities of perseverance, hard work, and responsibility.
- Make enough time for meals as a family. The parents should think of interesting topics of conversation and draw the children into the discussions.
- Provide nutritionally balanced meals. Plan for meals and keep in mind that breakfast is especially important. Also, children need protein to grow muscles as well as carbohydrates for energy and brain function.
- If your children do not have a servant's heart while accomplishing specific chores, instill a team mentality. At times, everyone together should help to get the work done no matter whose chore it is. In addition, they need to be taught to take initiative.
- Get to know their friends and welcome them in your home.
- Monitor carefully their television, movie, and computer time.
- Have regular family worship time. It does not have to be complicated. Some families read a small portion of Scripture at the dinner table as soon as everyone is

through eating. Then they share prayer requests, pray, and perhaps sing a song.

- Teach the value of reading good literature. This is helpful in both their school work and character. Start early in your child's life and schedule reading aloud on a regular basis.
- Have fun together. Children thrive on physical activity, and shared play forms a bond between parent and child. Some examples are family camping trips, board games, and throwing a baseball in the yard.
- Even work can be made fun and seem like play if a parent makes a game of it. Mothers can plan tea parties where their daughters learn the art of entertaining by doing something enjoyable together. Fathers can engage their sons as helpers when working on special projects around the house or in the yard. Plan adequate time for the project so everyone involved can relax and have fun participating.

Conclusion

For the child, the school-age years are a time of great growth physically and academically. This also can be a time to learn about God and the basics of how to study the Bible. Children can begin to understand at a more mature level their need for Christ.

They are usually eager to learn a variety of subjects and to please their parents. Let them begin to develop their own interests. Share in their joys, be gentle and kind to them, and have fun with them. Some children of this age, by God's grace, will become Christians. Whether the child is truly saved or not, continue faithfully to persevere "bring[ing] them up in the discipline and instruction of the Lord" (Eph. 6:4, adaptation added).

Questions for Review

1. To whom does King Solomon compare an old and foolish king?

2. What is Bible doctrine?

3. What are some of the practical ways to teach your children Bible doctrine? See Deuteronomy 6:4–9.

4. Answer the questions under the heading "Ask Yourself These Questions."

5. List at least four good deeds that your school-age child could do for others.

6. There are many ways for you and your children to praise God. Music is a primary way, but simply thanking God is also a good way. Look up the following verses and write out two examples for each Scripture of what you could teach your child to *think* in terms of being grateful to God.

   a. 1 Thessalonians 5:18

   b. Colossians 3:16–17

   c. Ephesians 5:19–20

7. How should you respond if another adult or even a child comes to you expressing a concern about your child's behavior?

8. Write out a simple time line beginning at creation and ending at the second coming of Christ and teach it to your child. Explain how the major Bible stories fit into the time line.

9. Prepare to teach your older school-age children how to use a Bible concordance. For example, look up *anger* and *hope* and list five to ten verses where these words are used.

10. What are the three main causes of conflict? Write out a brief way to deal biblically with each cause.

11. What Scriptures could you use to teach your child how to seek and/or grant forgiveness?

12. Read over the commonsense tips. Can you think of any others?

13. What is your prayer for your school-age child?

The Teenager

Most psychologists would likely agree with the following statement:

> In Western culture the transition from childhood requires passage through several years of adolescence, a period of life frequently acknowledged as the most troubled, the most stressful, and the most unpleasant of all stages of development.[1]

Well, how utterly depressing! The belief from the so-called experts is that teens *have* to go through a time of rebellion to gain their own identity apart from their parents. Certainly teenagers are thinking about life, what they believe is true, and what they want to do and become. If they are Christians, they can walk through that *maturing process* with grace and wisdom from God. If they are not Christians, they still do not have to go berserk!

---

1. Guy R. Lefrançois, *Of Children: An Introduction to Child and Adolescent Development*, 9th ed. (Belmont, CA: Wadsworth Publishing, 2000).

There is no separate category for the teenager in the Bible. According to Scripture, the child moves from older childhood into young adulthood usually around age twelve or thirteen. For many this sounds unthinkable, yet just over a hundred years ago here in America, people were often getting married in their teen years, working full time, and held totally responsible for their actions. In many other countries, even today, fourteen- and fifteen-year-olds are considered adults and may serve in war. Whatever the culture, there are certainly dramatic physical and social changes that take place during the average teen years.

Developmental Milestones

Usually the growth spurt for girls is earlier than for boys. Often girls are as tall and their feet as big as they are ever going to be by the time they are twelve or thirteen. Most will be a head taller than the boys in their class. Their hormones kick in and puberty is upon them. Girls at this age seem to have emotions as unpredictable as a compass in a magnet factory!

Boys, on the other hand, typically reach puberty around ages fourteen to sixteen. At that time, they grow several inches over a short period of time. Their physical strength increases and they delight that they are stronger than their mother and can joyfully tease her by grabbing her wrists to stop her from moving. By this time of life, they are (more often than not) looking down at their mom, and sometimes dad, from the advantage of greater height. Whereas girls' hormones are up and down, the boys' hormones are steady. Often they have the body and physical desires of a man yet, at times, can act like they have the brain of a pea!

Roles are changing and the teenager is moving toward independence. For most, there is a gradual alienation from parental control. They are intensely social and may even have their own language. What their great-grandparents would have said is *groovy*; what grandparents would have said is *cool*; what parents would have said is *awesome*; they would say is *sick*. Go figure! Adults who barely know how to use a cell phone, much less a computer, are amazed at how many teens today are experts at rapid-fire text messaging on cell phones. It almost seems that teens are born knowing how to easily do these things. The physical and social changes for teens are dramatic, but what do the Scriptures tell us?

The Biblical View of the Teenager

Solomon was David's son and became king of Israel during the time now known as the golden years of Israel's existence. Solomon was raised by a father whom God called "a man after my heart" (Acts 13:22). There was peace in the land after many years of turmoil. Solomon was rich, powerful, and famous. He could have anything he wanted, but when God asked him, "What would you like for me to do for you?" Solomon answered, "Give me wisdom."

Solomon needed wisdom to rule over his people, and God granted him that blessing. Later, God used Solomon to pen some of the wisdom literature in the Scriptures—Psalms, Proverbs, and Ecclesiastes. Because of the extraordinary gift God had given him, Solomon explains over and over again the way of wisdom as opposed to the way of a fool; he warns young people to listen to their fathers' instruction; he admonishes them not to be enticed by the "forbidden woman." He gives general truths about how to deal with an angry person, warns against strong drink, laziness, and a lying tongue. Of course, Solomon's admonitions for us to be wise apply to all age people, but there are specific instructions to the youth.

One such instruction is not to forget about God during this time of life. Even though Solomon was given supernatural wisdom from God, he did not always follow his own teaching. Probably the most famous example is in his having hundreds of wives. They must have come in all shapes and sizes and, for sure, they came in all varieties of religions. Even they could not make him happy, and in the despair of looking back over the vanity of his life, he warns:

> *Remember also your Creator in the days of your youth,* before the evil days come and the years draw near of which you will say, "I have no pleasure in them" . . . . (Eccl. 12:1, emphasis added)

The teen years are typically filled with activities. There are school and sports and parties and movies and video games, and part-time jobs for some. It often seems that every minute of every day is taken up with something other than the Lord. Sometimes teens are so busy that the parents have to say, "Hey, remember you have a family here!" It is no wonder, then, that they need to be reminded to remember God.

Teens are usually physically strong and have lots of energy. Solomon acknowledged this when he wrote, "The glory of young men is their strength . . ." (Prov. 20:29). That may be their temporary glory, but what really counts for now and for eternity is to know God through our Lord Jesus Christ and to be wise. Wisdom goes hand in hand with listening to instruction and heeding it. Even after a failure, the wise teen is correctable. Solomon appeals to them to remember that their wisdom begins with fearing the Lord.

> *To know wisdom and instruction*, to understand words of insight, to receive instruction in wise dealing, in righteousness, justice, and equity; to give prudence to the simple; *knowledge and discretion to the youth—Let the wise hear* and *increase in learning*, and the one who understands obtain guidance, to understand a proverb and a saying, the words of the wise and their riddles. *The fear of the LORD is the beginning of knowledge*; fools despise wisdom and instruction. (Prov. 1:2–7, emphasis added)

According to the Scriptures, teens *can* be wise and use discretion in the choices they make. Discretion means to be cautious. They *can* also, by God's grace, listen to God's Word with a view to obey. Since many teens are led by their feelings, it is especially important that they are taught objective truth from God's Word. Their parents might say, "Listen up!" Solomon put it this way, "Hear, my son, your father's instruction, and forsake not your mother's teaching, for they are a graceful garland for your head and pendants for your neck" (Prov. 1:8–9).

God, through Solomon, also knew that teens would be especially vulnerable to sexual temptation. They tend to make foolish, impulsive decisions. As a fish is drawn to the worm on the hook, the young man is drawn to the immoral woman. Solomon describes the scene:

> For at the window of my house I have looked out through my lattice, and I have seen among . . . the youths, a young man lacking sense . . . taking the road to her house . . . . the woman meets him, dressed as a prostitute . . . . She seizes him and kisses him, and with bold face she says to him . . . . "Come, let us take our fill of love till morning; let us delight ourselves with love." . . . With much seductive speech she persuades him . . . . All at once he follows her . . . he does not know it will cost him his life. (Prov. 7:6–23)

The Old Testament emphasis is for the youth to remember their Creator, have a reverential fear of God, and make wise decisions. To do that, they must learn to think objectively instead of by their feelings. Christian teens do not have to sin (1 Cor. 10:13). They can channel all their passion for life and energy for good. They can learn to love others and turn from their natural self-centered focus.

This is a time when teens are figuring out what they believe. Is it their faith or their parents' faith that they have? For many, it is affirmed as their own. For some, this may be the time that they (or you) realize they are unsaved. If unsaved, they may begin to evidence a life virtually lived for self. In addition to discerning their own beliefs, teens often face a daily onslaught of temptations and decisions. Whether they admit it or not, they need God and their parents to help them. While in the wilderness, in a speech to the Jews, Moses told them of God's help.

"The LORD your God who goes before you will himself fight for you, just as he did for you in Egypt before your eyes, and in the wilderness, where *you have seen how the LORD your God carried you, as a man carries his son*, all the way that you went until you came to this place." (Deut. 1:30–31, emphasis added)

God carried the Jew and he carries us today. Can we do less for our children as we persevere through their teenage years? One way that we *carry them* is that we are still responsible to discipline and instruct them in the Lord.

Discipline and Instruction in the Lord

The time for spanking is past. Parents must look to other forms of discipline for the teen. Sometimes simply telling them what they did wrong is sufficient, that is, if they are wise. There are blessings for those who listen and learn from a reproof because "whoever heeds reproof is honored" and "is prudent" (Prov. 13:18; 15:5).

If your son or daughter will not listen, then their discipline might be removal of a privilege, loss of certain possessions, or restrictions from certain activities. For instance, a young teenage girl who uses her cell phone to place forbidden calls to an older boy would lose her privilege of having a cell phone. The cell phone, for this girl, is a provision for her flesh. In other words, the cell phone provides a ready temptation to defy her parents' instruction. The biblical basis for removing her privilege is to "put on the Lord Jesus Christ, and make no provision for the flesh, to gratify its desires" (Rom. 13:14).

To "put on the Lord Jesus Christ" is to think and act as the Lord would.

The teen years are a time for parents to give their children more and more freedom but also a time for letting them deal with the consequences of their choices. Often, this is the hardest thing for parents to do, especially the moms. Martha's husband, Sanford, explains it this way:

Consider the balance required for a seesaw to stay level with the ground. You can overload either side and it will tip down. The heavier the load on one side, the faster the balance will be upset and the faster that side will come crashing down, a bad consequence. Not only will overloading one side make it tip faster, but moving the load of one side of a balanced seesaw farther out from the center will make it crash faster. How much freedom a parent gives a child has to be balanced by how trustworthy, obedient, and mature of character the child has been in the past. This requires the parent to know his child and exercise wisdom.

When a child builds up trust on one side it should be balanced by more freedom on the other. If the child *does* act trustworthy but is not given commensurate freedom, he will come crashing down into resentment. If the child *does not* act trustworthy but is given too much freedom he will crash down into disrespect and poor choices. Many aspects of parenting require the parent to wisely discern the amount of trust and freedom necessary to balance the child's growth into maturity.

As the teen gets older, the parent will usually find the child wanting and willing to take on more and more freedom. It is the parent's job to raise up that child so that he will exhibit mature trustworthiness appropriate for that increasing freedom.

Increasing freedoms could be in the form of a part-time job, going to the mall with friends, or going on a campout with only older teens and no adult present. The balance is never just right, but is always moving up and down this way and that, because parents and children inevitably make mistakes. We might give just a little too much freedom, and they may not be as trustworthy as necessary at any given point. As the seesaw starts to swing, we reign in or adjust as necessary to keep balance. Thus, discipline must be appropriate to not tip the seesaw out of balance. Remember, ultimately the child is going to leave home and be legally free in the eyes of the society/legal system. Will he be mature and trustworthy enough in character to balance his freedoms in that adult role? The parent's job of childrearing is to, as faithfully as they can, prepare the child to be let go.

Sanford's seesaw illustration is especially helpful for parents who have a child-centered home and think they are being merciful to the child when, in fact, they are being foolish by not holding their child responsible. It is also helpful for parents who are over-controlling and fearful. Both need to pray for wisdom and perhaps receive counsel from their elders at church if they are unsure of how much freedom to give or not give.

A key element in bringing up teenagers is your relationship with them. "If possible, so far as it depends on you, live peaceably with all" (Rom. 12:18). The teenage years are a revealing time, sort of "displaying more of what's on the inside." This means that all kinds of fleeting thoughts enter their minds. and sometimes, to the horror of their parents, they speak them. Often those thoughts pass on as fast as they came. So, be careful as parents to inquire about the thoughts but don't take each one too seriously. Remember that this is a time of change from commanding to advising. Therefore, be as flexible as you can about their choices but unbending when it comes to the moral will of God.

In moving toward an adulthood relationship with your teenager, don't forget that there are two sinners involved in the relationship, not just one. Be a godly model to them by "speaking the truth in love" (Eph. 4:15). Talk with them and treat them as you would want to be treated. Be humble and admit when you are wrong. Take an interest in their world and what they like.

One father whose son is very gifted musically lets his son play in a Christian music group. The words they sing are honoring to the Lord but the music, in the father's estimation, is dreadful. Is the style of music a hill to die on? Some parents would say, "Absolutely, Yes!" Others would say, "No, and I like the music!" The point we are trying to make is this: be as flexible as you can, enjoy your teenagers, and, like the father in the music illustration, give them as much freedom as you can, balanced out by their trustworthiness. (Oh, and by the way, attend the concerts, even if you have to wear earplugs!)

Now let's turn our attention to what to do when the teenager is manipulative or disrespectful. Even though we have touched on this subject in previous chapters, we want to give a fuller explanation here.

Dealing with Manipulation and Disrespect[2]

When teenagers are disrespectful or manipulative, they are not honoring their parents. They are using unbiblical

2. For further information on helping angry teens, we recommend: Lou Priolo, *Getting a Grip: The Heart of Anger Handbook for Teens* (Amityville, NY: Calvary Press, 2007).

words and/or their countenance to bully the parent into let-ting them have their way. If that does not work, the teenager will often punish the parents in some way such as giving them the cold shoulder or walking off in anger and slamming their bedroom door. They are acting in many ways like the Bible describes a fool.

A fool takes no pleasure in understanding, but only in expressing his opinion. (Prov. 18:2)

The way of a fool is right in his own eyes, but a wise man listens to advice. (Prov. 12:15)

Better is a poor person who walks in his integrity than one who is crooked in speech and is a fool. (Prov. 19:1)

It is an honor for a man to keep aloof from strife, but every fool will be quarreling. (Prov. 20:3)

Do you see a man who is wise in his own eyes? There is more hope for a fool than for him. (Prov. 26:12)

Whoever trusts in his own mind is a fool, but he who walks in wisdom will be delivered. (Prov. 28:26)

A fool gives full vent to his spirit [anger], but a wise man quietly holds it back. (Prov. 29:11, explanation added)

When teens act like fools they won't listen and are wise in their own eyes. Sometimes they are angry and cruel, and always they are determined to have their own way. Often their folly escalates and the parents are left confused and/or angry

113

themselves. When that happens, you have two fools talking to each other! Instead of answering back as a fool would, parents are to give an answer that will convict their child of what is wise.

> Answer not a fool according to his folly, lest you be like him yourself. (Prov. 26:4)

Parents answering like a fool might explode in anger, or beg their child to be nice, or cry because their feelings are hurt. They would likely defend their position to the child at length. In the process of the conversation, parents would likely forget the original issue and be led off in the smoke screen of a departure from the original subject.

The teen wants to have his own way, and if he cannot, he can at least make everyone within earshot miserable. So, instead of answering back as a fool would, parents should calmly give the teen an answer so that he will not be "wise in his own eyes" (Prov. 26:5).

> Answer a fool according to his folly, lest he be wise in his own eyes. (Prov. 26:5)

The following chart gives examples of how manipulation and disrespect might escalate on the part of a teen told by his parents that he cannot borrow the car.[3] When he first asks to borrow the car, there is nothing wrong with the request. It is only when told "no" that his true heart's motive comes out.

---

3. Adapted from the chapter on manipulation in Martha Peace, *Damsels in Distress* (Phillipsburg, NJ: P&R Publishing, 2006), 59–72.

MANIPULATION PLOY	PARENTS AND TEENAGE SON
1. Sweet talk	1. "Mom and Dad, may I borrow the car tonight to go with my friends to the movies?"
2. Beg	2. "Mom, Dad, *please* let me go (follows them around begging). All my friends are going and I'll be the only one who can drive us. If I don't go they won't get to go either. *Please*!"
3. Cry	3. Tears in his eyes. "Let me take the car. I promise I'll be careful."
4. Anger	4. Yelling in anger, "Why won't you let me go?" Stomps out of the room and slams his door. His parents can hear him throwing things around in his room.
5. Cold Shoulder	5. Refuses to speak to either of his parents but gives them a cold stare when they try to talk to him.
6. Accusations	6. "You're not fair!" "I thought I could depend on you." "You don't love me." "You're being selfish." "You're doing this deliberately to embarrass me in front of my friends."
7. Threats	7. "I hate you. I can't wait to get away from you." "I will leave here and you will never see me again." "I'll go anyway no matter what you say."

Now consider the following chart with the parents' answers to their foolish son.

MANIPULATION PLOY	PARENTS AND TEENAGE SON	AS HIS FOLLY DESERVES
1. Sweet talk	1. "Mom and Dad, may I borrow the car tonight to go with my friends to the movies?"	1. "No son. We're sorry but we think it best you stay home tonight and rest for school tomorrow."
2. Beg	2. "Mom, Dad *please* let me go (follows them around begging). All my friends are going and I'll be the only one who can drive us. If I don't go they won't get to go either. *Please!*"	2. "Son. We're sorry but this is a wisdom issue and we think it unwise, so you need to stop begging me. How should you have responded when we said, 'no'?" (See Proverbs 4)
3. Cry	3. Tears in his eyes. "Let me take the car. I promise I'll be careful."	3. "Son, your responsibility is to graciously take 'no' for an answer and to repent from demanding your way." (See Proverbs 18:2.)
4. Anger	4. Yelling in anger, "Why won't you let me go?" Stomps out of the room and slams his door. His parents can hear him throwing things around in his room.	4. "Son, you are using anger to try to get your way and to punish us. Instead, you should show love to God by honoring our decision and be grateful to God and to us that you can take the car on occasion." (See Matthew 22:36–39.)
5. Cold Shoulder	5. Refuses to speak to his mom but gives her a cold stare when she tries to talk to him.	5. "Son, you are still using unbiblical means to manipulate me to get your way. This is not right. What you are doing is sinful and you are to stop." (See Ephesians 6:2.)

6. Accusations	6. "You're not fair!" "I thought I could depend on you." "You don't love me." "You're being selfish." "You're doing this deliberately to embarrass me in front of my friends."	6. "Son, you are responding foolishly. You say you are a Christian, and if you are you should see our decision as God's will for you. Your responsibility is to graciously and gratefully give in." (See Colossians 3:17.)
7. Threats	7. "I hate you. I can't wait to get away from you." "I will leave here and you will never see me again." "I'll go anyway no matter what you say."	7. "You are being very malicious. If you do those things, it *will* be difficult for us but God will give us the grace to endure it and you will face the consequences of your sin." (See Proverbs 18:7.)

Any time your child uses unbiblical means to try to get his way, he is sinning. When this happens, you are likely to have very unpleasant emotions: fear, confusion, frustration, or guilt. These emotions will make it difficult for you to respond without sinning (defending yourself, blowing up in anger, foolishly giving in, overreacting with discipline). Therefore, it is important to work diligently to learn how to respond calmly and wisely (giving the fool the answer he deserves).

If you become confused at any point in the conversation, say, "I need to think about what I want to say. I'll be back." Then go somewhere and write down the conversation: "I said . . . ," "He said . . . ," "I said . . . ," "He said. . . ." Once

117

you have the conversation written down, go over it point by point and make sure you are not responding like a fool and that you are giving the fool an answer so that he won't be wise in his own eyes. Then go and say, "Remember when I said . . . ? That's not what I should have said, this is what I should have said . . . ." The more you work at thinking factually instead of responding emotionally, the more you will honor God and the better you will become at showing love to your children by trying to help them see their responsibility.

All Is Said and Done in Love

When you are engaged in a verbal battle with your teenager, remember that "the anger of man does not achieve the righteousness that God requires" (James 1:20). If the shoe were on the other foot and you were the one acting like a fool, think about how you would want someone to reprove you. Speak in a kind, gentle tone of voice because "love is patient and kind" (1 Cor. 13:4). Ask the Lord to help you and, if necessary, excuse yourself to go pray and practice aloud what you want to say. Have as your heart's desire to be like the Lord Jesus Christ who never spoke in sinful, unbridled anger or foolish proud defense of himself. He always perfectly showed love for God and for others even when (and especially when) they were sinning. "Do nothing from rivalry or conceit, but with humility count others more significant than yourselves. . ." (Phil. 2:3). You should be more concerned about God's glory and trying to help your child than you are determined to out-bully him.

118

So, learn to speak the truth in love and be assured that regardless of how much your child is wise in his own eyes, you can keep "a good conscience, so that, when you are slandered, those who revile your good behavior in Christ may be put to shame. For it is better to suffer for doing good, if that should be God's will, than for doing evil" (1 Peter 3:16–17).

What If They Outright Rebel?

When a teen outright defies your biblical guidelines, it is time to pray and act carefully. As we have said previously, make sure you have the facts. If it is your teen's word against someone else, be cautious. You do not want to automatically assume that your child is guilty or that he is innocent. Perhaps there are other witnesses or extenuating circumstances that could help you decide what to do. One time when Stuart and Zondra had some difficulty with one of their children, they asked a few elders from their church to interview both them and their children to see whether there were areas that needed attention. If need be, get counsel from your church leaders and deal with any known or disclosed sin in your own life (Matt. 7:1–5).

If your teen is a professing believer, then he is also your brother in the Lord. Clarify to him what he is doing wrong and exhort him to repent and give God glory. Use Scripture, which "discern[s] the thoughts and intentions of the heart," to validate your reproof and have as your motive to "*restore him* in a spirit of gentleness" (Heb. 4:12; Galatians 6:1, emphasis added). If he will not repent but still claims

119

to be a Christian, then follow the steps of church discipline in Matthew 18:15–17.

The Lord has a twofold purpose in church discipline: one is to put godly pressure on the erring brother to repent for his own good and God's glory, and the other is to keep his church pure. You can use the same discipline principles in your home as well. The first step is to go to the child privately. If he repents, it is the end of the matter. No one else need ever know. If he does not repent, take one or two witnesses with you and confront him with his sin. At this stage, if he repents, it is the end of the matter. If he does not, then go to the church leaders and explain that you have already done the first two steps. They will then investigate, and if they fully practice church discipline they will "tell it to the church" (Matt. 18:17). The purpose of this would be for the church family to lovingly exhort their errant teen brother to repent. If, after a time, that does not happen, then the pastors would tell the church family that the unrepentant person is to be considered as an unbeliever.[4] Some churches do not discipline teens until they reach age eighteen because they cannot be a member until then. If this is the case or if the church does not fully practice church discipline, take it as far as you can and then treat your professing but unrepentant teen as an unbeliever because he is living like one.

When considering discipline for your erring teen, move in stages. Make sure you have all the facts from both sides. Then the first step in discipline for most parents is to start removing privileges. This will be a judgment call on the part

4. Public announcements (the third step of church discipline) are for members of the church, and typically a member must be eighteen years old to join.

of the parent, and certainly you should pray for wisdom. The next step is placing them on restriction. Perhaps because of their lack of being trustworthy, they simply need to be home with Mom and Dad. For the rebellious teen to stay at home, parents should consider the possible harmful influence he or she has on his siblings. Sometimes it is wise to place them somewhere else temporarily, perhaps with a relative or family in your church.

If teens are still rebellious and will not listen, you can place them somewhere else for a longer period of time, such as a boarding school for troubled teenagers. There are also some Christian-run residential organizations that would be one step away from juvenile hall, if the teen is willing to cooperate.[5] As a last resort, realize that what your rebellious teen is doing may be illegal. At least in some states if not all, it is illegal for your teen to be ungovernable. When it gets to the point where the teen may be a safety threat to himself or others and/or is doing illegal things, it is time to get the police involved.

One of God's provisions to protect the young person out of control as well as protect those around him is the legal system. The police and courts have been given authority from God.

> Let every person be subject to the governing authorities. For there is no authority except from God, and those that exist have been instituted by God. (Rom. 13:1)

5. Several of these facilities profess to be evangelical. Every parent (with the help of the church leadership) should evaluate each facility carefully to see what each requires, what it teaches, etc., before enrolling their child. An example of a crisis counseling ministry that helps individuals and families is Twelve Stones Ministry in Helmsburg, Indiana (www.twelvestones.org).

This is a very grievous step and not to be taken lightly, but very well may be the right thing to do. For example, if your child is using drugs and stealing money, it would be better for him to be arrested and placed in juvenile jail than to continue to place himself, his family, and his community at risk. Any witnesses, and often this is the parents, have a moral obligation to try to protect the child and to protect others from him. As embarrassing as it would be for the parent and the teen, there are many youth who have turned from a life of crime to become mature, functioning adults. The parents need to be humble enough to come forward as witnesses with the underlying motive of restoring their child and giving God glory.

Continue to be faithful to present the claims of Christ and the hope of the gospel. But unless and until they are saved, keep appealing to their consciences to do what is right. Take comfort from the Lord that every day you endure a rebellious teen and show love to him, you are showing love to both your child and to God, because love "does not rejoice at wrongdoing, but rejoices with the truth," and "love . . . endures all things" (1 Cor. 13:6–7).

Helpful Commonsense Tips

- Be available to talk with your teen even if the timing is inconvenient for you.
- Remember, teens love to have fun. Smores, Silly String attacks, water guns, and huge ice cream cones go a long way.
- Be sure to have enough food to eat as they will seem to be always hungry.

- Take special caution with their freedoms on the computer and with their cell phones. Computers need pornography and address filters. Parents should also occasionally check behind teens to see what web sites they are accessing.

- If your teen drives an automobile, you might want to consider one that does not go super fast.

- Teens should be part of the family and not spend hours and hours alone in their rooms with the door shut.

- If they struggle with mathematics and you can help them, re-explain for them the type problems they had in class. Then have them, without your help, do their homework. Afterward, check it and you will see what problems they missed and why. Then re-explain by making up new practice problems and instruct them to work the problems they originally missed. That way you can be sure they understand it for themselves and you are not doing their homework, but they are!

- For the teen who does not organize his schoolwork well, help him with a calendar for the semester. For example, use the syllabus of the class and write in all the tests and projects on the due dates. Fill in any dates that should be special study days or project research days. Keep those dates in mind and follow up with your teen. Do that each semester until he is trustworthy to organize the work by himself.

- Since it will not be long before your teen leaves home, make sure he is skilled at basic household chores such as cooking and washing clothes.

- Teach your older teen how to do his budget, and give him a checking account. Deposit enough money every month so he can pay for gas, car insurance, social activities, and school expenses. Teach him how to balance his checkbook and enroll him in a Christian money management course.

- If your teen has a part-time job, it should not consume his life such that he has no family or church time or is so tired he cannot function well in school.
- Most of the teen's social life should be in group settings. Single dating, except on rare occasions, provides too many opportunities to be tempted sexually.
- Develop a common interest with your child whether the interest is related to Christianity or not. If they don't know the Lord, they would at least have something you could enjoy together during their teen years and when they are grown.
- If your child is wavering in his faith or rebelling, read the thirty-day devotional in chapter 10.

Conclusion

The teenage years do not have to be as unpleasant as most psychologists think. Not even all unbelieving teens rebel but, if they do, there are many biblical resources to help parents. It is a time of life for teens to gradually earn their parents' trust and move toward further independence.

Love them, enjoy them, and take an interest in what interests them. Pray for them (without ceasing!) and be faithful to the Lord whether your child is or not. Teenagers do not need to rebel to *find themselves*. What they need is the Lord.

Questions for Review

1. For what did King Solomon ask God? What books of the Bible did Solomon write?

2. Even Solomon's many wives could not make him happy. What does he warn young people about in Ecclesiastes 12:1? What does Solomon encourage them with in Proverbs 12:13?

3. According to Proverbs 1:2–7, what is the beginning of knowledge and what do fools despise?

4. What is the biblical basis for disciplining your teen by removing privileges?

5. According to the seesaw illustration, what should the parent try to balance?

6. When your teen is disrespectful or manipulative, he is acting like a fool. List several proverbs that describe a fool.

7. How might you answer back like a fool?

8. Instead of answering back like a fool, you should give your teen a biblical answer that he deserves, so he won't be wise in his own eyes. Write out how you should answer from the following foolish manipulative responses.

   a. Having tears in her eyes and begging to go to the movies with her boyfriend.

   b. Saying, "I hate you and can't wait to get away from you."

   c. Saying, "You have always loved my sister more than you loved me."

d. Saying, "You are not fair."

e. Yelling in anger, "I want to go and you can't stop me."

f. Saying in a cruel, calculated way, "I wish you were not my father!"

9. When your child is manipulating you and acting like a fool, what should you do if you become confused?

10. What are the biblical means to use if your teen outright rebels?

11. What are some common interests that you could cultivate with your teenager?

12. Read over the commonsense tips. Which ones do you need to work on? Can you think of any others?

13. What is your prayer for your teen?

8

Parents Who Provoke

Picture this typical biblical counseling scene: Mom, Dad, and their child are sitting around the pastor's desk, opposite the pastor. The parents have brought the child to seek help for his terrible problem with anger. They cannot cope with his blowing up anymore. Mom is crying and Dad is sitting back in the chair, arms folded with a fed-up look on his face. The mom is trying to mediate between the teen and her husband.

As the parents tell the story of how their child behaves, the teen either says nothing or has an ugly, angry retort. All three (and perhaps the pastor, too) are at their wits' end. Although the child *is* responsible to God for his behavior, let's consider what else may have unnecessarily provoked him to anger. Two Scriptures are clear about the subject:

Fathers, *do not provoke your children to anger*, but bring them up in the discipline and instruction of the Lord. (Eph. 6:4, emphasis added)

Fathers, *do not provoke your children*, lest they become discouraged. (Col. 3:21, emphasis added)

Both of these passages speak of sinful actions of the parent. The Greek word for *father* can at times be translated *parents*.[1] The father has the greater responsibility, but both parents can provoke their children. This command is about habitual actions that over time have this effect on the child. It is not a rare event but a way of living. This is not referring to a parent who says or does something once or a few times, and the child does not like it and becomes "wrathful." This is repeated provoking so that over time the child becomes angry and *loses heart*.

The biblical counterpart to this discouragement is to "bring them up in the discipline and instruction of the Lord" (Eph. 6:4). One way to do that is to encourage your children. Think of the Lord Jesus speaking to the seven churches in Revelation 2 and 3. He often starts with encouragement, then addresses their sinful tendencies, and closes with more encouragement. Some ministers say the balance should be eighty percent encouragement and twenty percent correction.

Although everyone is responsible for his or her own sin, and nothing the parents do permanently determines the child's reaction, parents should want to make it as easy

1. James Strong, *The New Strong's Concise Dictionary of the Words in the Greek Testament* (Nashville: Thomas Nelson, 1995), 69 (#3962).

as possible for the child to think and do the right thing. Let's consider some parenting styles that provoke children to anger.

The Proud Parent

A *proud parent* probably takes first prize in the category of provoking children. They will not admit when they are wrong. If their child lovingly dares to tell them they are wrong, the child is severely scolded or punished for not honoring the parent. A proud parent lives a hypocritical life. The message to the child is loud and clear, "Do what I say but not what I do!"

These parents often humiliate the child privately or in front of others. There is a lack of concern and sensitivity toward the child (or anyone else). Often their most important concern is what others think about them. Their pride blinds them to their own culpability, and it is almost impossible for them to admit they have done anything wrong. Proud parents will not listen to counsel—it is always someone else's fault. They are often blind to their sin, but God *does* oppose the proud (James 4:6; 1 Peter 5:5).[2]

Most often such a proud parent is not a believer. The good news is, God also "gives grace to the humble" (James 4:6b). So if the proud parent humbles himself and repents, there is great hope for change. He or she can receive a new kind of heart that can learn to put off pride and put on humility.

2. For further study on pride and humility, see: Stuart Scott, *From Pride to Humility* (Bemidji, MN: Focus Publishing, 2002).

The Despairing Parent

The despairing parent is one who feels sorry for himself. Often he or she plays vain regrets over and over in the mind. All is doom and gloom. Things are hopeless, it's always too late, and there is no hope for recovery. Those around this kind of parent are often asking, "What's the matter? What's wrong now?"

No one enjoys being around these parents, not even their children. The "glass is half empty, poor me" kind of parent greatly exasperates a child. The parent is often stuck in the "why are you cast down, O my soul, and why are you in turmoil within me?" mode instead of the "hope in God for I shall again praise him, my salvation and my God" mode (Ps. 42:11). It would not occur to *the despairing parent* to be thankful or hopeful or to give the child hope no matter what has happened. They will not be able to reassure their child that God will see them through and, for the believer, use it for good in their life to make them more like Christ (Rom. 8:28–29).

The Controlling/Angry Parent

Proud and despairing parents are not the only ones who provoke their children. The *controlling/angry parent* does, too. These parents are overly authoritarian. They use angry words and a harsh/ugly tone of voice to bully their children into behaving a certain way. Often they "lord it over" their children instead of lovingly lead them. This type of parent does not forbear with people. "Forbear" simply means putting up with differences. Instead, a controlling/angry parent has the view, "It's my way or the highway!"

They are not kind and patient, and they are selfish as they only prefer one way, theirs. They are not like God who is "gentle, open to reason, full of mercy . . ." (James 3:17). They are like the man who is wrathful and creates a lot of "clamor" (Eph. 4:31). They are *not* "quick to hear, slow to speak, slow to anger . . ." (James 1:19). They do not remember that "the anger of man does not produce the righteousness that God requires" (James 1:20). They have not learned how, by God's grace, to put off anger and put in its place kindness, a tender heart, and forgiveness (Eph. 4:31–32).

It is very provoking for a child to live under this kind of manipulation and lack of love. Often at first, the child is simply afraid of the parents' reaction. It is confusing because the child never knows what will or won't set the parent off in an angry tirade. Eventually, the child will probably become embittered and angry. Over time, the child is very likely to *lose heart.*

The "Guess What the Rules Are Today?" Parent

Next there is the *guess what the rules are today? parent.* For the child, the rules and the consequences often change. There may be too many rules for anyone to keep up with, or they can just be unenforced or enforced only sporadically. Think about it this way: what would you do at work if the policies kept changing or they were only sporadically enforced? It would be exasperating even to try to please your boss. You would most likely give up trying. Well, the same applies to a child. Certainly it is not wrong to have family standards, but there needs to be wisdom behind them, consistency, and consideration for mercy in upholding those standards. Selfishness, laziness, or weariness can lead a parent to keep changing the rules. But God says, "Do not be slothful in zeal, be fervent in spirit, serve the Lord." He encourages us to "not grow weary of doing good, for in due season we will reap, if we do not give up" (Rom. 12:11; Gal. 6:9).

The Exaggerating Parent

There is also the *exaggerating parent.* These parents think and talk in terms of "always, never, everyone, a million times." Instead of dealing with each individual matter separately, they lump everything at once into the conversation. The result often becomes something untrue. This provokes the child and distracts from the focus of what they *have* done wrong.

Exaggeration may make a more dramatic point, but it is simply one form of lying. Instead of lying or generalizing to the point of lying, we are to "put away falsehood . . . [and] speak the truth with [our] neighbor" (Eph. 4:25, adaptation added). People, including children, *can* change in concrete, specific ways. Sweeping exaggerations only exasperate them. Instead, stick to the issue and be kind in your tone. This reminds us of the letter Paul wrote to Timothy with instructions to be "correcting his opponents with gentleness. God may perhaps grant them repentance leading to a knowledge of the truth, and they may escape from the snare of the devil . . ." (2 Tim. 2:25–26).

132

The "Must Be Perfect" Parent

The *must be perfect parent* promotes a standard that is impossible to meet. This is driven by the parent's own pride. It's ironic, though, because the parent himself cannot be perfect. So, he becomes an instant hypocrite. The child's room may be as clean and neat as is humanly possible, but the parents' hearts are likely to be either puffed up in self-righteous pride or provoked to despair because no matter what the child does, it is never good enough. These parents are like the Pharisees in that "they tie up heavy burdens, hard to bear, and lay them on people's shoulders, but they themselves are not willing to move them with their finger" (Matt. 23:4).

Parents like this tend to miss opportunities to encourage their children because their focus is on the most minor imperfections. If their child does not simply rebel against the parents' impossible standards, the child is at risk of becoming so performance-driven that he judges everyone else by these outward, impossible standards. That would be a child any Pharisee would be proud to raise! Have standards as you teach your children, but have at the heart of your parenting style the hope of gospel-centered grace that is offered to imperfect people.

The "Fear of What My Child and Others Might Think" Parent

Another category of the provoking parent is the *fear of what my child and others might think parent*. This can paralyze parents from making appropriate decisions. The parent's thoughts tend to be "if I do that, he won't love me" or "if I make him face the consequences of his sin, he will never forgive me" or "what will other people think of me and my parenting?" This is a self-serving and foolish way for a parent to think. The concern should be "What would achieve God's righteous end?" instead of "Oh, dear, what is my child going to think about me?" Like Paul, they must learn to live "not to please man, but to please God who tests our hearts" (1 Thess. 2:4).

This kind of fear and foolish lack of confidence is very provoking for a child. You see this when a spoiled two-year-old pushes his mother away in anger when he does not get his way and, even more sadly, when the seventeen-year-old is quickly bailed out of jail after being arrested for drunken driving. Parents should be more concerned about God's glory and the child's good than they are intimidated by their child's anger or negative opinion of them. This naturally leads us to the next category of provoking parent.

The Submissive/Easily Manipulated Parent

The *submissive/easily manipulated parent* actually encourages and teaches the child to sinfully persist in getting his way, because often the parent will foolishly give in. The parent should be loving and compassionate yet execute discipline when needed, along with appropriate consequences.

Parents like this are often confused or embarrassed by their child's reaction, so they take the easy way out and give in for the sake of "peace" (this is not true biblical peace). In a previous chapter we taught what to do if your child is manipulative or disrespectful. Although it is tempting to defend yourself or give in for the sake of peace, those reactions are not biblical parenting. The parent is being manipulated and responding foolishly. This reinforces the child's disrespectful behavior because he learns that if he perseveres hard enough and long enough, he will either get his way or at least make everyone miserable in the process. Often children with easily manipulated parents *are* angry and spoiled.

The *submissive/easily manipulated parent* must learn to "be strong in the Lord and in the strength of his might. . . . stand firm" rather than succumb to the child's sinful manipulation (Eph. 6:10–13). If the parent does not biblically stand up to the child in love, at least to some extent, the child has been unnecessarily provoked.

The "Why Can't You Be Like Your Brother?" Parent

Children are not the only ones who can manipulate; parents can, too. Sometimes they try to manipulate a child into better behavior or better grades by being a *why can't you be like your brother? parent.* We are confident there were times that Mary, the mother of Jesus, at least thought about saying to her other children, "Why *can't* you be like your brother?" But there is probably not a child on the planet who—upon hearing "*why can't you be like your brother?*"—does not at least momentarily in his heart go the way of Cain.

Parents cannot help but notice differences in their children. Children can be widely different in personality, strength and weakness of character, intelligence, self-control, and talents. Children need help and guidance from their parents for all their weaknesses, but parents should stick to "speaking the truth in love" (Eph. 4:15). No children need parents to point out that they are not as good as their brothers. The standard is God, and if the child's weakness is a sin, show him grace by giving him the gospel and, if necessary, biblically disciplining him.

The "Let Me Live the Life I've Always Wanted through You" Parent

It is clear that Christian parents must discipline and instruct their children for sin issues, but what about being raised to be a star baseball player or a missionary? Sometimes this is the parents' dream, not the child's. This is the *let me live the life I've always wanted through you parent.* What interests the child is secondary to what the parents have their hearts set on. These parents are living vicariously through the child, so they either ignore or are not interested in what the child might like. This is not "in humility count[ing] others more significant than yourselves" (Phil. 2:3b, adaptation added).

Children have God-given abilities, and parents should encourage them in their abilities as much as possible. Carter is a six-year-old who is musically gifted and makes up songs on the piano. One of his compositions has four movements! So, he is now taking piano lessons. His great-aunt who is a concert pianist is hopeful that he will follow in her footsteps. However, it remains to be seen whether Carter will have the self-discipline to seriously practice like his Aunt Paula. It is not wrong to encourage Carter's talents, but for Aunt Paula or Carter's parents it would be wrong to provoke him into losing heart because it is their dream come true and not Carter's. They need to keep in mind that God may have a different plan for Carter's life.

The "Hands-off and Let the Child Decide" Parent

The *let me live the life I've always wanted to live through you parent* is too hands-on. Conversely, the *hands-off and let the child decide parent* is too uninvolved. These parents rarely if ever discipline or instruct their child. The parents may be lazy or they may not really know their responsibility is to "bring them up in the discipline and instruction of the Lord" (Eph. 6:4).

They let their children make decisions that the parents should be making, such as where to go to church—and sometimes whether to go to church at all. It's ironic that this category of a provoking parent would never let their sick children decide whether they wanted to go to the doctor, but when it comes to deciding what is best for the children spiritually, the parents want to please their children so much that they unwisely give in to the child's preferences.

Often parents will become convinced that their church is in serious error, yet they will stay at the church because their child is comfortable there. After the child is grown, the parents will leave for a doctrinally solid church. Just as parents should never let their sick child decide whether to go to the doctor or not, Christian parents should never let their children decide which church to attend. Should parents listen to their child's reasons for wanting to go to a church? Yes, but the burden for the decision is placed by God directly on the parents' shoulders.

Some other decisions children should not be allowed to make are whether to go to school, whether to be kind, whether to eat with the family, or whether to be safe. A *hands-off and let the child decide parent* risks making a foolish mistake and provoking the child to anger.

The Tradition- or Culture-Driven Parent

The *tradition- or culture-driven parent* elevates family tradition to the level of a command of God. While it is all right to have cultural traditions and family traditions, it's not all right to elevate them to the level of Scripture as the Pharisees did (Matt. 15:9). Like the Pharisees, some families raise their traditions to be equal to or more important than God's Word. Keeping those traditions becomes a mark of spirituality. One family we know has homemade pizza each Christmas Eve, and they all gather for the occasion. We wonder what will happen when the oldest daughter marries and her husband's family has a Christmas Eve tradition of the candlelight service at church followed by a dinner of pork roast and figgy pudding (whatever figgy pudding is!). All the children should be taught to leave and cleave and make their own family traditions.

Long before children leave and cleave, teach them that these traditions are wonderful and we love them, but it's all right if other families do things differently. Teach them that the nonnegotiables are God's timeless commands and principles. Teach them that it is okay to lovingly exercise freedom in the Lord as, "For freedom Christ has set us free; stand firm therefore, and do not submit again to a yoke of slavery" (Gal.

5:1). Do not provoke your child to anger by being a *tradition-* *or culture-driven parent.*

The Omniscient/Presumptuous Parent

The *omniscient/presumptuous parent* thinks he knows what his children are thinking. These parents judge motives and assume the worst. They do not bother to gather data to defend their position, which makes them foolish, since Scripture warns us, "If one gives an answer before he hears, it is his folly and shame" (Prov. 18:13). This is confusing to a child and greatly exasperating.

Often this kind of parent will tell the child, "You did that deliberately to hurt my feelings," when the child did what he did because he is a sinner and has folly in his heart. It would not have mattered who the parent was! Parents should stop thinking they know a child's motives. Only God can know motives. It is when Christ comes back that he will "disclose the purposes of the heart" (1 Cor. 4:5). Those disclosures, by the way, will not only be the child's motives but also his parents' motives. Do not presume. Do hear the matter fully. Do consider your child's appeal if it is given respectfully. Sometimes we parents try to play God, but we are not God and we are not all-knowing.

I (Stuart) remember, after instructing our twelve-year-old son Marc to drink only one soft drink a day, hearing two cans open in the kitchen after a hot day of work in the yard. I just "knew" he was going to drink them both. Just as I was gearing up for the reprimand, he came around the corner with two glasses of soda—one for him and one for me. I confessed my sin of presumption to God and thanked my son for his thoughtfulness. It was good that I didn't have the chance to act on my presumption because an *omniscient/presumptuous parent* often grievously provokes his children.

The "If Love Is There, It Is a Secret" Parent

This may be shocking to some of you, but it is possible for parents not to love their children. We call this person the *if love is there, it is a secret parent*. When parents are selfish, impatient, unkind, self-absorbed, cold, and aloof, they really may only love themselves. Some parents do not show affection to their children. Neither do they tell their children that they love them. Saying, "I love you" is a start, but showing it by your deeds is the proof. The apostle John describes biblical love in one of his letters: "Little children [believers], let us not love in word or talk but in deed and in truth" (1 John 3:18, explanation added). We are to love our neighbors, and our children are among our closest neighbors!

The "Preoccupied by So Many Things" Parent

The *preoccupied by so many things parent* does love his children, but is overly busy. These parents may be doing lots of good things, but there is little time for the children. When Martha became a Christian, she was teaching nursing full time. Her children would come home from school full of excitement about their day, but by the time Martha got home, they had forgotten most of what happened and were busy doing other things. It was only after she quit her job to be home with her family that she realized what she had missed.

Instead of being so busy that you hardly notice your children, get off the phone or the computer. Turn off the television. Cut out something you are doing. Take the time to share in their lives by listening to their little joys and sorrows. Learn how they think and give them wise guidance. Do this with warmth and love. Enjoy the time you have with them. Take Paul's advice:

> Look carefully then how you walk, not as unwise but as wise, *making the best use of the time*, because the days are evil. (Eph. 5:15–16, emphasis added)

We have seen several ways that parents provoke children to anger and discouragement. If you realize that you have been provoking your children in one or more of these ways, what should you do?

The answer is simple: humble yourself before God and before your child. To humble yourself before God means you sincerely confess your sin to God, willingly take corrective steps, and ask his forgiveness. Trust in his promise that he will be "faithful and just to forgive us our sins and to cleanse us from all unrighteousness" (1 John 1:9).

To humble yourself before your child means you sincerely confess your sin to your child and ask his or her forgiveness. Don't be fuzzy or vague or make light of the sin by saying, "It was a mistake." Call sin what it is and say, "I was wrong, will you forgive me?" Clearing your conscience with a child you have wronged is a serious and urgent matter. Consider the Lord's words:

"So if you are offering your gift at the altar and there remember that your brother has something against you, leave your gift there before the altar and go. First be reconciled to your brother, and then come and offer your gift." (Matt. 5:23–24)

Conclusion

Although there are times that a young person is sinfully angry without being provoked by a parent, there are many parents who do provoke their children. Both parent and child must assume responsibility for their actions, but a provoking parent holds the greater responsibility in the breakdown of unity. Remember the parents at the beginning of this chapter who took their angry child to the pastor for counsel? The pastor should hear all three of their perspectives on the situation. He knows that no parent will be perfect in all the above ways, but faithfulness is what God wants, Christ-centered faithfulness.

To whatever degree the parents provoked their child, the pastor must, by God's grace and for his glory, call them to repentance. He must exhort them to change from being a provoking parent to being a wise, biblically encouraging parent. If they love the Lord and their child, they will.

Questions for Review

1. What things can provoke a child/teen to anger?

2. What things from the list above are problems or could be problems in your parenting?

142

3. What specific actions (words, deeds, etc.) do you need to put off for each thing listed above (#2)?

4. What specific actions can you put on as the right alternative to each thing listed in question #2?

5. What specific thoughts/desires might contribute to each of your wrong actions in # 2?

6. What new thoughts/desires can you put on for each of the thoughts in #2? See Appendix D for help in doing this.

7. Write out a prayer. In it thank God that you are not doing "all" the ways that could provoke a child. Ask God for his help to change.

8. What should be your motivation for being a better parent?

9. If you are clearly a provoking parent, with whom can you pray and make yourself accountable for change?

PART THREE

The Persevering Parent

Moreover, it is required in stewards that one be found faithful. (1 Cor. 4:2, NASB)

For you have need of endurance, so that when you have done the will of God you may receive what is promised. (Heb. 10:36)

9

Special Cases

I t is often helpful for parents in special situations to encourage one another. It is even more important for these parents to receive the right kind of instruction and support from their local churches. They need to know that God has both the wisdom and grace they need. They need to know that they must still honor God's Word in their special situations. But they also need to know that others will not burden them further with unreasonable standards or rash judgments.

The Pharisees were the religious leaders in Jesus' day. They preached from and studied the Old Testament scrolls that we know as the Old Testament, which contains the law of God. Focusing sinfully on looking good outwardly, the Pharisees made up hundreds of practical applications to God's law. The problem was that they elevated their applications to the level of the law. Those *supposed* laws are called the Talmud.

Even today Christians must be careful not to raise an application of a command or biblical principle to the level of the law of God. Often "a" way becomes "the" way and then turns into "God's way," when there is actually freedom in the Lord. For example, children are told in God's Word to "honor your father and mother" (Eph. 6:2). Some have suggested that when the child wants to talk with his parent and the parent is talking with someone else, the child should place his hand on the parent's hip instead of interrupting. Now that *is* a good idea! However, although it is only "a" way, it can quickly become "the" way and then turn into "God's way" of honoring parents.

Of course, biblical commands and clear principles must be obeyed. They *are*, if you will, "Thus saith the Lord!" Parents are to wisely and individually apply the biblical principles to their *own* children's lives. Otherwise they run the risk of being like the Pharisees. That's what legalism does. It focuses on outward adherence to rules instead of "weightier matters of the law" such as love and compassion (Matt. 23:23).

Our main purpose in this chapter is to suggest some of the "a" ways to apply biblical principles to special cases in parenting. Our attempt is not exhaustive, as entire books could be written on each of these topics. But we did want to provide some practical tips and resources for special cases. The special cases we will address are single parenting, divorced parents sharing the children, blended families, one parent being gone a lot, one parent being saved and the other not, grandparent problems, and children with special needs. (As important as it is, we chose not to deal with adoption. An exhaustive treatment of that topic has been done recently by Russell Moore).[1] Let's begin with the first special case.

1. Russell D. Moore, *Adopted for Life* (Wheaton, IL: Crossway, 2009).

Single Parenting

A single parent is on duty 24/7. Often single parents have no one to back them up if they are delayed getting home from work or come down with flu. It is common for single parents to struggle financially, and often they will have discipline problems. A single parent is going to need help at times.

Often the help comes from the Lord through their families, friends, or churches. They must feel free to call on elders/pastors to help them. In solid churches that really care for their congregations, the leaders take seriously the biblical admonition to "[keep] watch over your souls." These leaders know they will "have to give an account [to God]" for the way they care for their flocks (Heb. 13:17). Pastors should check up on single parents to find out how they are doing. Do they need help? What are their specific needs? How are they doing spiritually? How are the children doing? The single parents also have a responsibility to ask for help.

Asking whether the single parent needs help *and* the single parent asking for help is a two-way street. It is critically important that the single parent be humble enough to request help. Also, he or she must be willing to be held accountable and follow counsel. It may be that when the elders give counsel, the parent thinks of a better way or at least a biblically acceptable alternative. The elders must give the single parent freedom in the Lord as long as the parent is not violating biblical principles.

Suppose a single mom seeks counsel from the elders because she is unsure about changing jobs. There are pros and cons, and she is confused. Often, the pastors think of something the single mom had not. Together with her, they can pray and consider what biblical principles are involved. For instance, a biblical principle is to "seek first the kingdom of God and his righteousness . . ." (Matt. 6:33). The new job is easier for the mom physically and it pays more money, but the down side is that she and the children would miss church every other Sunday. The elders should explore the possibilities and suggest an alternative, biblical plan of action, along with offering the support and help necessary to implement it.

Single parents need to have a budget. Often they may not know how to make one or how to adhere to it. They may already have incurred debt. The pastor does not have to teach the single parent how to handle these issues, but he could refer the parent to someone (usually in the church family) who can help. One of the biblical principles to follow in this case is to be a wise steward of what the Lord provides, but there are many practical ways to implement it.

If you are a single parent who is biblically free to marry and looking for a spouse, it is often wise not to get the children involved until there is the likelihood of an engagement. One single mom we know dated the man who is now her husband only on the weekends her children were visiting their father. That way, the children and the suitor did not become attached to each other in case the relationship did not work out. The underlying biblical principle would be, "Let each of you look not only to his own interests, but also to the interests of others" (Phil. 2:4). However, as we have said, there are many practical ways to implement this principle.

Single parents must be wise concerning close attachments to people of the opposite sex. This may include their pastors, other people's husbands or wives, or co-workers. When you are hurting emotionally, it is easy to tell your problems to another. It is equally easy for that other person to feel sorry for you and want to help you. This kind of intimate sharing can lead to devastating heartache for many people including the single parents' children. So another important biblical principle is to "make no provision for the flesh, to gratify its desires" (Rom. 13:14). Certainly, there is a reason why Paul instructed young widows to remarry! It was to keep them out of trouble. Anyone who needs to meet with someone of the opposite sex to discuss problems should have a witness present. Often it would be the pastor's wife or a godly older woman in the church family. Single parents must guard their hearts and protect the hearts of the men or women around them.

Many times single parents have to work outside the home, but they should be careful not to allow others to take over the responsibility of raising their children. The single parent, even if it is the mother, is to be the spiritual leader in the home. He or she should have regular family devotions with the children in order to "teach them diligently" (Deut. 6:7). This could be as simple as reading a small portion of the Bible at the supper table, which could generate discussion or questions. If unsure what to say, the single parent can always say, "Well, I'm not sure about the answer to that question but I'll find out." Then the family can pray together. The biblical principle underlying this is to bring up the children in the "instruction of the Lord" (Eph. 6:4).

I (Stuart) remember my father gathering us together regularly for family devotions. I tried to do the same with my family, but was not as regular as he. Those times around God's Word when I was young lent great stability to our family and strengthened our view of God. Although a formal time of family worship is not commanded, it would help single parents and their families to fear and trust the Lord.

Taking the children to church should be a priority. Single parents (all parents, for that matter) should be careful not to allow extracurricular activities for themselves or their children to take them away from each other so much that there is almost no family time. Although most extracurricular activities are not sinful, some can consume your lives. An example might be certain levels of sports competition. Instead, be wise about commitments. One biblical principle to consider is "making the best use of the time, because the days are evil" (Eph. 5:16).

While single parents are a special case in parenting, they often find themselves in another special case:

Divorced Parents Sharing the Children

Several years ago, a young wife and mother called her mom and said, "My husband has told me that he is leaving me. There is another woman involved, but what I want to know right now is if my children will be all right." Her mother, who had been through similar circumstances, said, "If you do not become embittered or use your children in an emotional way to make you feel better or them feel sorry for you, they will very likely be fine."

It is not only all right but it *is* right for children to continue to love the parent who has left them. What a *divorced parent sharing the children* should want to accomplish is to teach the children biblical principles that will help them love the erring parent and yet also be discerning. Children need to learn to think through their situations biblically. It's okay for them to love their sinful parent. Keep in mind that God loves us in spite of our sin. How many details they need to know about the divorce depends on their ages, but they *never* need to know the sordid details. When the time is appropriate they should be told that the erring parent loves them, but that he (or she) also loved his sin more than he loved the family. Stress that it would not have mattered who his family was—the sin problem is in his heart. Then the faithful parent can explain that they all need to pray that God would grant repentance to the other parent. Face the reality of the situation and be honest with them, and do not promise that their wayward parent will come home. He might or might not.

When a divorced parent is upset with the ex-spouse, he or she should not use their child to vent how he feels. The child is helpless to do anything about it and could become greatly distraught. He would, perhaps, even feel hatred in his heart toward his other parent. As the child matures and sees hypocrisy and character weaknesses in the erring parent, the godly parent must help the child to honor the sinning parent and overcome evil with good (Rom. 12:21). A child *can* live in the reality of the other person's sin and not disrespect him. You must be able to talk about the real issues and then help the child respond in a biblical manner. This can be done without slandering the other parent or gossiping. Help children to think and act biblically.

If something is going on in the other home that concerns the parent such as drunkenness, immorality, drugs, child molestation, or abuse, the godly parent should foster an attitude in his or her home that makes it easy for the child to be open. That way the child will be comfortable coming to the parent with concerns. Believe the child and take measures within your

153

ability to correct the issue. Seek pastoral counsel and legal counsel if needed. Let the children have a means to contact you if they are fearful or in danger. Perhaps they should have a cell phone. If your child is upset or distraught and believes himself to be in danger, then go get him. If necessary, get the police involved. The laws of our land are one of the resources that God uses to protect children because "every person [is to be] subject to the governing authorities. For there is no authority except from God, and those that exist have been instituted by God" (Rom. 13:1, adaptation added).

Keep in mind that some children will use the situation of divorced parents to get whatever they want. They will play one parent against the other or threaten to live with the other parent if they do not get their way. Both parents need to be discerning and investigate the facts. Otherwise, they risk taking up an offense for the child without hearing the other side of the story. "The one who states his case first seems right, until the other comes and examines him" (Prov. 18:17).

Both parents need to be more concerned about what is best for the child than they are about getting even with the ex-spouse. They should support each other as much as possible. If, on the other hand, it is impossible to work through what is best for the child then obtain legal intervention. The biblical principle here is: "If possible, so far as it depends on you, live peaceably with all" (Rom. 12:18).

What if the child comes home from visitation and is upset and angry because of something the other parent said about you? Suppose the father tells them, "Your mother never loved me and she kicked me out of the house even though I did not want to leave." Well, suppose the other side of the story is that the dad was committing adultery and moved in with

154

another woman even though the mom told him she was willing to forgive him and work toward reconciliation. The children have only heard their dad's side. So they return home upset with their mom. In such a situation it would be time to calmly sit down and have a family meeting. Mom should remind the kids that they must be respectful in their tone of voice but that she wants to hear what happened. Let each child have a say. Then Mom should factually and calmly tell them the truth. If they do not believe her, she can offer to have witnesses talk with them. The witnesses should be people who love them and are grieved over how their dad acted but still pray for his repentance. When upsets are handled orderly and lovingly instead of in a hysterical and chaotic manner, the children will learn quickly to check the other side of the story. Some of the biblical principles here are: "If one gives an answer before he hears, it is his folly and shame," "Let love be genuine. Abhor what is evil; hold fast to what is good," and "Let each one of you speak the truth with his neighbor" (Prov. 18:13; Rom. 12:9; Eph. 4:25).

Sometimes a person who is coping with being a *single parent* later becomes a *divorced and sharing the children parent* only to remarry and become part of the special case of a *blended family.*

Blended Families

When a man and woman plan to marry and blend their families, they should undergo specific premarital counseling. The counseling should be biblical and very practical. Once married, the couple's priority must be on the marriage rather than the children. This will take time and work, because prior to remarrying their focus was just the children. This will be a huge adjustment for the adults and the children but, by God's grace, can certainly be achieved. The underlying biblical principle is: "Therefore a man shall leave his father and mother and hold fast to his wife, and the two shall become one flesh" (Eph. 5:31).

The newlyweds should set the precedent of being a team in parenting. They should decide what the standards are in the home and, when necessary, appropriately discipline the children. Often the mother will not let her new husband make decisions for or discipline her children, and the new husband can be guilty of the same problem with his children. Sometimes a former spouse will not want his or her kids to be disciplined by the new stepparent. Regardless, godly parents should prayerfully and with underlying biblical principles in mind, figure out together how to proceed and present a united front. Stepchildren should be taught that their stepfather is still head of the home and responsible for what goes on there and for them when they are in his care.

At first or if wrong habits have already been formed, parents of blended families may need to seek counsel from their pastor or elders or a biblical counselor. Three key commands they may need help in applying are, "Now as the church submits to Christ, so also wives should submit in everything to their husbands," "Husbands, love your wives, as Christ loved the church and gave himself up for her," and, "Children, obey your parents in the Lord, for this is right" (Eph. 5:24, 25; 6:1).[2]

2. For a detailed explanation of what it means for the husband to lead his family and for the wife to submit biblically, see Stuart Scott, *The Exemplary Husband* (Bemidji, MN: Focus Publishing, 2002) and Martha Peace, *The Excellent Wife* (Bemidji, MN: Focus Publishing, 1999).

Both parents need to make a concerted effort to get to know the other children and love them. They can learn to love those in whom they put their treasure (time, energy, money, and affections). Don't play favorites. Love them all and plan special things for the entire family and for each child individually. Be interested in their interests. One stepfather we know is often seen playing ball in the yard with his stepson. He serves on the youth committee at church so that he can be with his three teenage stepchildren during youth activities. Although he now has children of his own, an outside observer would not be able to tell which ones are his biological children. He loves the Lord and he loves his wife and he loves all the children in his home. He takes seriously the biblical mandate to lead his little flock. His wife takes seriously the biblical mandate to leave and cleave and be a godly helper—suitable for her husband.

Be wise by supervising children of the same age range of the opposite sex. Beware—they can be physically attracted to each other. Set new precedents as a couple when you realize that you need them. One newlywed couple realized that both of their children were accustomed to coming freely into the bedroom of their parent. So, in an effort to get them used to something different, they told the kids that a closed door meant they could knock only if there was some urgent reason. One day, the mom was showering and the stepdad was getting dressed when a telltale little knock was persistent at the door. It was the mom's two-year-old son. His stepdad asked, "What is it?" The child replied, "I want to come in." The stepdad then asked, "Is this something that can wait?" The child replied, "No, I want to tell you that I love you." Well, almost instantly the door was opened very wide for that little boy to come in and get a big hug from his new stepdad! In that home, the Lord is helping all nine of them to adjust *and* there is a lot of love.

When One Parent Is Gone a Lot

A parent may be gone a lot because of a job, the military, being in jail, or other reasons. Often it is the mother who is left to pick up the slack. If an emergency comes up, she should by all means try to talk with her spouse. Otherwise, she should find a trusted, biblically minded woman to give her counsel. The underlying biblical principle would be from Titus 2:

> Older women likewise are . . . to teach what is good, and so train the young women to love their husbands and children . . . that the word of God may not be reviled. (Titus 2:3–5)

The younger woman, perhaps with the help of the older woman, should seek to make the kind of decision that she thinks her husband would make. That way, even if her husband cannot be part of the decision-making process, the wife would maintain the spirit of the marriage bond, that the husband is still head of the home. When she is able to communicate with her husband, she can tell him the decision she made and that she thought it was what he would have decided. If it is not what he would have done, he should tell her but keep in mind that she tried.

The at-home spouse and the absentee spouse should communicate as much as possible. It is easier today with cell phones and computers but, of course, the absentee spouse may be hindered from communicating at all. The absentee father needs to make a concerted effort to be involved with his wife and children as much as possible even from a distance. Neither party should indulge in self-pity and brooding. If the one at home needs help, he or she should seek help and guidance from their church family. While one spouse is absent, both should be wise in the company they keep. It would be easy to fall into sexual temptation and justify it because no one would know. Instead, they need to avoid temptation as well as the appearance of evil since their marriage vows are in effect whether together or separate.

> Flee from sexual immorality. Every other sin a person commits is outside the body, but the sexually immoral person sins against his own body. Or do you not know that your body is a temple of the Holy Spirit within you, whom you have from God? You are not your own, for you were bought with a price. So glorify God in your body. (1 Cor. 6:18–20)

When it is close to time for the absent spouse to come home, the at-home spouse needs to update him or her. If it is the husband, he should listen to all that has transpired before exercising his vocal leadership, especially because "If one gives an answer before he hears, it is his folly and shame" (Prov. 18:13). In a similar way, an absent wife should ease back into her role. If the father is absent, the mom should teach the children that when he comes home they will all look to him for guidance and decisions. Children should be taught that the leadership role of the father is a good thing. It is God's will for them.

The at-home spouse should make it a happy day of celebration when the absent spouse comes home. Recently Martha sat next to a soldier on a plane as he flew home from a war zone. He was going to see his wife and firstborn child, who was two weeks old. While he expected to see his wife and parents at the airport, he was met by what looked like half his hometown. There were banners and cheers and cameras flashing as he walked to his wife and took the baby in his arms. What a happy day for that young couple! By the way, Martha walked right past the people picking her up because she was crying too hard to see them.

The absence of one parent is a difficult special case, and so is it when one parent is saved and the other is not.

When Parents Are Unequally Yoked

The wife whose husband is unsaved is to practice the principles of 1 Corinthians 7:12–16 and 1 Peter 3. She is to evangelize her husband not with words and gospel tracts stuffed in his pillow, but with her "respectful and pure conduct" (1 Peter 3:2). Like all wives, she is to show biblical love, respect, and submission to her husband unless he asks her to sin. She should enjoy him, think of him as someone special to her—someone beloved—and think of ways to please him.

The believing wife (or husband for that matter) is to refuse to sin if her spouse wants her to do so. God's authority always overrides a husband's authority in the case of a sin issue. The believing spouse should seek as much influence over the children as possible, but not turn the children against their unsaved parent. Show respect to the other spouse in front of the children as well as behind the other spouse's back. This does not mean you live in a pretend world, ignoring the unsaved spouse's sin. Children, especially as they grow older, will notice. Talk with them privately and teach them that their unsaved parent has no capacity to love God as they should. They should pray for his or her salvation and not expect the unbeliever to think or act like a Christian. The saved parent should, when necessary, lovingly and respectfully reprove the unsaved spouse by appealing to his or her conscience to do what is right.

The husband of an unsaved wife needs to be forbearing and as flexible as possible short of sinning. He is to love her and live with her in an understanding way (1 Peter 3:7). The unbelieving spouse has to be pleased to live with the believer, or he or she can leave (1 Cor. 7:12–16). If the unbelieving spouse departs, it should be because the spouse was Christ-like and committed to the marriage and not because he or she was impossible to live with. Both spouses, if possible, should seek pastoral/biblical counsel for those very difficult matters.

We touched on what to do if one spouse is unsaved, but what if one spouse *professes* to be a Christian and yet his life does not show it? This is a common problem. Many adults have prayed salvation prayers and go to church, yet do not have a reconciled relationship with the Lord. This is demonstrated by their lack of love for God or joy in serving him. They are like the false teachers in Titus 1:16 who "profess to know God, but they deny him by their works." Others in their church family accept them as saved because they do not know them well. But at home it is another story. Even if their salvation is suspect, it is only the church elders who have authority to treat sinning spouses as unsaved, and then only after going through the whole church discipline process in Matthew 18. The Lord

Jesus himself said of an unrepentant so-called believer, "Let him be to you as a Gentile and a tax collector" (Matt. 18:17). This means the church has made public to the church family that he is to be treated as an unbeliever and put out of the church if he does not repent.

Because individual spouses do not have the church's authority, they must assume the sinning spouse is saved and hold the other to his profession until the church acts. This means the husband or wife of the erring spouse must first follow the steps that the Lord laid out. If this is your situation, go to your spouse and, in love, tell him his sin in specific terms with a scriptural basis. Implore him to repent and give God glory. If he or she listens and turns from the sin, it is the end of the matter. No one else need know. The following are the steps in the church discipline process as our Lord Jesus laid them out:

> "If your brother sins against you, go and tell him his fault, between you and him alone. If he listens to you, you have gained your brother. But if he does not listen, take one or two others along with you, that every charge may be established by the evidence of two or three witnesses. If he refuses to listen to them, tell it to the church. And if he refuses to listen even to the church, let him be to you as a Gentile and a tax collector." (Matt. 18:15–18)

The underlying purposes of church discipline are to keep the church pure, to protect the Lord's reputation, and to allow the entire church family to pray for and exhort the brother or sister to repent. This is one way that brothers and sisters in the Lord, including husband and wife, help each other become as much like the Lord Jesus as possible.

162

If the "professing" spouse is not part of any Bible-believing, disciplining church and will not turn from sin, the believing spouse should practice as much of the process in Matthew 18:15–18 as he or she can. At some point the saved spouse, with the help of church leaders, should be able to conclude that *if* the spouse were part of a Bible-believing church, he would be put out of the church and treated as an unsaved person. This can give the Christian freedom to consider and treat the spouse as unsaved. Another underlying principle here is:

> Whoever says "I know him" but does not keep his command-ments is a liar, and the truth is not in him, but whoever keeps his word, in him truly the love of God is perfected. By this we may be sure that we are in him: whoever says he abides in him ought to walk in the same way in which he walked. (1 John 2:4–6)

Spouses can have problems with each other, but couples can also have problems with other family members such as grandparents.

Grandparent Problems

It is commonly known that previously normal parents lose their minds upon holding that first grandbaby in their arms! Not only do they lose their minds, but they start to have opinions. Firm opinions. This is not to say that some of their opinions are not good, because often they are. Wonderful, in fact! So, young couples would be wise at least to consider their parents' opinions. However, although they must remember to show respect to their parents, they do not have to obey them.

163

What they must do is leave mother and father and cleave to each other.

When lovingly standing up to their parents, grown children should be as forbearing as possible, but firm when the Scriptures instruct otherwise or when they believe something different is best. Some areas that often cause conflict are spanking, permissiveness, spoiling grandchildren, allowing endless cartoon watching, what church to attend, where to live, undermining parents' authority, and taking up an offense for the child without hearing the parents' side of the story.

When young parents stand firm against their parents' counsel, the grandparents may react sinfully. They might pout or withdraw because they feel hurt. Or they might become angry and offended. If this happens, the young couple should fear God more than man. Scripture says, "For am I now seeking the approval of man, or of God? Or am I trying to please man? If I were still trying to please man, I would not be a servant of Christ" (Gal. 1:10). Grandparents who try to control sinfully don't tend to give in graciously, so be prepared to revisit issues with them on occasion. Be as flexible as you can. It is not going to hurt children in the long run to skip vegetables one time at their grandparents' house and then have ice cream. Ultimately, though, most grandparents will come around to the young couple's views. If not, seek pastoral counsel.

There are grandparents who, instead of being overly involved, are not involved enough. This is certainly unbiblical, and their adult children should explore the reason why. Unless the grandparents would be extremely poor examples, try to persuade them to be more involved. Invite them to your home more often. If they continue to be uninvolved, do not let your family's happiness depend on their involvement.

You might want to find some other godly grandparents and "adopt" them so you and your children will have the benefit of a grandparent-type relationship.

Most grandparents are afraid to say something if their children or grandchildren are doing anything wrong. However, they should humbly and lovingly express their concerns. Young parents, on the other hand, should make it as easy as possible for the grandparents to express their opinions or give a reproof. One underlying biblical principle is: "A fool despises his father's instruction, but whoever heeds reproof is prudent" (Prov. 15:5). Grandparents need to learn what it means to be godly. Parents need to learn what it means to leave and cleave. They all should strive together to be "eager to maintain the unity of the Spirit in the bond of peace" (Eph. 4:3).

Now let's turn our attention to the last special case, when the child has special needs.

When the Child Has Special Needs

This material was adapted with permission from Dr. Laura Hendrickson's chapters in *When Good Kids Make Bad Choices*.[3]

All children are created by God, and we are to love and respect them as part of creation. This includes children who are impaired. As a reminder that God would help him speak to Pharaoh, God told Moses, "Who has made man's mouth? Who makes him mute, or deaf, or seeing, or blind? Is it not I, the LORD?" (Ex. 4:11). Children, impaired or not, are precious

3. Elyse Fitzpatrick, Jim Newheiser, and Laura Hendrickson, *When Good Kids Make Bad Choices* (Eugene, OR: Harvest House, 2005), chapters 6 and 7 and Appendix C. Appendix C has helpful information concerning medications.

to God and an instrument in his hand for the Christian parent's spiritual growth and ultimate blessing.

It is no accident that you have the children you have. God has an all-wise and good purpose behind giving them to you.

> And we know that for those who love God all things work together for good, for those who are called according to his purpose. For those whom he foreknew he also predestined to be conformed to the image of his Son, in order that he might be the firstborn among many brothers. (Rom. 8:28–29)

Those who *love God* are Christians and are being obedient to God's Word. God's *purpose* is always his own glory. *All things* are the good and the bad things that happen to us, the good days as well as the difficult days with our children. Somehow, someway, God uses all that happens to us to help us become more and more like Jesus Christ. Now *that* has to be the ultimate blessing!

As we saw in an earlier chapter, children are born with folly in their hearts. This includes the special-needs child. They are born rebelling against the God of the Bible. Their hearts are bound by sin and limited by sinful desires and choices. They are like King David when he acknowledged that from the womb, he was "brought forth in iniquity, and in sin did my mother conceive me" (Ps. 51:5). David did not mean his parents were being immoral, but that he was a sinner from conception.

Depending on the special need of the child, the parents will most certainly have special challenges. For example, it is easy to help the very bright and self-disciplined child with his homework, but what about the child who is developmentally

166

delayed? Or how easy is it to help the child who is autistic or "predisposed in his makeup to be inattentive"?[4]

Whatever the special challenge, what do the Scriptures tell us about the child and the parents' response? How the parents respond to their child and how the child responds to others is best described as a biblical balance. The balance is between compassion and loving instruction with correction of the child.

Dr. Hendrickson explains the compassion side of the balance this way:

> Ultimately, those of us who have kids with special challenges have the same goal as all other parents. We want to set a gentle but uncompromising standard of obedience to God's commands before our children, understanding their special areas of weakness, and always pointing them to the cross for the power to live the way that God commands.
>
> Psalm 103:13–14 says that "as a father shows compassion to his children, so the LORD shows compassion to those who fear him. For he knows our frame; he remembers that we are dust." God's standard for our behavior is always high, but because he understands our weaknesses, he gently and patiently enables us to achieve his standard by his grace. Let's seek to model our parenting after our Father's example.[5]

It would easily be a temptation for parents to excuse or minimize bad behavior because they feel sorry for their child. On the other hand, it could also be a temptation for some parents to respond with impatience and anger when their child struggles with bad choices or slow learning. But Dr.

4. Ibid., 108.
5. Ibid., 114–15.

Hendrickson tells us, "When we take a hard-line approach, we are failing to temper our justice with mercy."[6]

Research your child's challenge and learn from other parents and medical experts what has been shown to be helpful for your child. But balance your compassionate understanding with all of what the Scriptures teach. The Scriptures are clear that children, even those challenged in some way, are responsible for their sin.

One young couple we know had a child who was severely challenged and would require a great deal of speech therapy. They knew that if they did not discipline their child as they did their other children, he would not only be a very unhappy, spoiled child, but would have so many behavior problems that he would likely not cooperate with the therapy. Because his parents obeyed the Lord and disciplined their child in love, their son progressed a lot further than anyone thought he would. A challenged child who is brought up in the "discipline and instruction of the Lord" is much more likely to be attentive to teachers and to respond socially to others than a child who is not disciplined (Eph. 6:4). His life, although difficult, will be much better than a child who has not learned self-control and does not listen or patiently try.

Parents as well as their challenged children *can* honor and glorify God. Neither one, if they know the Lord, has to go through the difficulties in vain. The Lord will use the challenge to teach them, to reveal his grace to them, and to bring himself praise. So, by God's grace, seek to maintain a biblical balance between compassion and discipline and instruction. (See Dr. Hendrickson's chapters in *When Good Kids Make Bad Choices*.)

6. Ibid., 109.

Conclusion

This chapter has been about certain special cases. We have tried to give you examples of "a way" to apply biblical commands and principles to these situations. There is no problem, however large or small, that cannot be helped by the Lord and his Word. Whether you are a single parent, or part of a blended family, or deal with controlling grandparents, God's grace is sufficient to give you guidance and wisdom. Whether divorced, temporarily separated from a spouse or raising a special-needs child, God understands, will help you, and intends for his church to come alongside to assist you. None of those difficult situations can keep any parents from being faithful to the Lord and to their child.

Questions for Review

1. Do you find yourself or someone close to you in a special situation? What?

2. What are God's resources to help you as a parent? Do you have any additional resources?

3. Considering the situation(s) you cited in question #2, what things can you be doing that are faithful?

4. Are there any areas of your life and/or parenting where you have rationalized your sin because of your special case? If so, what do you need to do about it?

5. How is God using the circumstances of your special case for good in your life?

6. If you need additional help from others, what would it be? Have you made your needs known to the church? Why or why not?

7. Are there friends or other parents in your church whom you can assist in their special cases?

8. Is there any way you have been using your children wrongly? For example, to vent your anger, to emotionally take the place of your spouse, to send messages to an ex-spouse, to play favorites in a blended family, etc.?

10

When Things Don't Go as Planned

The best thing a parent can do is live in awareness that he is the Perfect Father's child, in need of him every moment. There may be times on our parenting journey, though, that we become painfully aware of this fact. If God has allowed an ongoing trial with your child, however bad it may be, it is also a truly *good* thing. It is good because, through it, God intends to reveal himself and to accomplish much for you, your child, and his glory. Whether a son or daughter is physically or mentally challenged, making disastrous decisions (pregnancy, drugs, etc.), actively rebelling, or just living a spiritually bankrupt life, our Lord and Savior is greater than any of these things and can see us through as parents.

One of the most difficult things a Christian parent may face is for their maturing young person to reject the gospel and depart from the faith he has grown up knowing about,

171

and perhaps even professing to believe. This chapter is written with those parents in mind. If you are such a parent, you are not alone, although it may sometimes feel like it. There are many others in your situation, and your heavenly Father has not abandoned you. Nor has he given you more than you can handle by his grace. The following is a month's worth of daily devotions that can offer you encouragement, biblical direction, and examination.

Day 1: Keep trusting God in the dark times

In difficult times we must always fall back on who God is and cling to those truths. He is good (Ps. 119:68). He is perfect in all his ways (Ps. 18:30). He has not failed you, nor is he indifferent to your pain (Isa. 63:9). He is faithful (Ps. 145:13). God is all-wise and all-knowing (Ps. 139:1–24). God is light, and in him is *no* darkness *at all* (1 John 1:5). Deuteronomy 32:4 gives us a good summation of these truths:

> The Rock, his work is perfect, for all his ways are justice. A God of faithfulness and without iniquity, just and upright is he.

One of the most difficult things to place in God's hands can be our children. To agree with God's timing and/or decision concerning the salvation of our children is a matter of sheer faith and trusting submission. Be careful how you question God during these times. "Why God?" can be either a cry for understanding or an angry response to your circumstances.

Parenting years are a special time to trust the Lord. Trust means that we are willing to have the attitude of Job when he accepted calamity as well as good from the hand of God. Job lost everything dear to him in one fell swoop. But he initially had two astounding reactions to his extreme trial: he still worshiped God, and he did not judge God. This is the kind of love and trust that we can have, too.

> Then Job arose and tore his robe and shaved his head and *fell on the ground and worshiped.* And he said, "Naked I came from my mother's womb, and naked shall I return. The LORD gave, and the LORD has taken away, blessed be the name of the LORD." *In all this Job did not sin or charge God with wrong.* (Job 1:20–22, emphasis added)

Similar to Job, Habakkuk resolved that even if "everything" was gone (food, job, savings account, etc.), he was going to trust proactively in God who works all things according to his perfect will. God can give you grace to do this as well (Heb. 4:16).

> Though the fig tree should not blossom, nor fruit be on the vines, the produce of the olive fail and the fields yield no food, the flock be cut off from the fold and there be no herd in the stalls, yet I will rejoice in the LORD; I will take joy in the God of my salvation. God, the Lord, is my strength; he makes my feet like the deer's; he makes me tread on my high places. (Hab. 3:17–19)

Let these two men be a great example to you of trusting God in your situation.

173

Day 2: "Draw near to God, and he will draw near to you." (James 4:8)

What a precious promise from God! Think for a minute about the far-reaching implications of this verse in every area of your life! Specifically as parents, though, we must go to God when we are perplexed and hurting, pour out our hearts to him (Ps. 62:8), and make our requests known (Phil. 4:6). We can go to him and "[cast all our] anxieties on him, because he cares for [us]" (1 Peter 5:7, adaptation added). He is near to the brokenhearted (Ps. 34:18), and he is near to those who see their sin and repent (James 4:8–9). The best thing we can do is draw near.

> But for me it is good to be near God; I have made the Lord God my refuge, that I may tell of all your works. (Ps. 73:28)

Think of life as a classroom with God as the teacher. God is always present, and never needs to send in a substitute. If we are saved by his grace, he is always there to help us! What a privilege we have to be able to cry out to God.

> God is our refuge and strength, a very present help in trouble. Therefore we will not fear though the earth gives way, though the mountains be moved into the heart of the sea . . . . (Ps. 46:1–2)

Day 3: Where do hope and joy really lie?

Our real hope and joy must be in God alone: in who he is and in his promises to us. Do you still have hope and joy in him? Our hope is what we are depending on and what we have set our heart's desire on as an absolute "must have." Parents who truly hope in God alone will not live in despair over their children. Hope anywhere other than in the Lord *will* disappoint you, but hope in Christ "does not put us to shame, because God's love has been poured into our hearts through the Holy Spirit who has been given to us" (Rom. 5:5).

Many of us don't realize how far our little tentacles of hope have stretched until we are tested. There once was a time when we (Zondra and Stuart) realized that we were actually placing hope in:

- Our children's salvation and blessedness.
- Our whole family increasing in godliness, togetherness, and joy.
- Others seeing us as amazing parents.

Instead, as parents we must set our hearts and hopes on God alone, knowing that he *will* help us and he *will* walk with us (Heb. 13:5–6).

Where we place our hope is where we find (or try to find) our ultimate joy. No matter what is going on, you can have joy in who Christ is, what he has done for you, how he is God to you, and the promise of heaven with him forever—*if* these are where your hope lies.

Children can bring us great sorrow if they are rejecting Jesus Christ and/or acting foolishly to their detriment. But it *is* possible, and even imperative, to have sorrow *and* joy. Although there is a place for humble (not bitter) sorrow, we are to turn from a focus on self or circumstances and think more about God, his daily goodness, and his undeserved grace.

> As servants of God, we commend ourselves in every way: by great endurance, in afflictions, hardships, calamities . . . *as sorrowful, yet always rejoicing*; as poor, yet making many rich; as having nothing, yet possessing everything. (2 Cor. 6:4, 10, emphasis added)

Day 4: Be thankful in all things

When things are difficult, thank God for anything you can think of: for who he is, for his ability and willingness to help you, and for everything he has done for you in your situation. Thank him for all he is doing to mature you and for allowing for your good, even if it is hard and you don't understand. Be thankful for his perfect work in you. Thank him for showing you how much you need him. Thank him that he is all you need.

Being thankful is a fruit of the Spirit. It can mean the difference between spiraling downward into self-pity, depression, and acts of sin, or moving upward to allow God to strengthen, encourage, and focus you on his will and glory. Make a Thankful List and rehearse it. Any time you are in a hurry and feel angry, bitter, disappointed, or discontent, list five to ten things for which you can thank God. When you have more time, expand that list to include twenty-five to fifty things for which you are thankful. Be as specific as possible. You can always start with thanking God for your own salvation!

Give thanks in all circumstances; for this is the will of God in Christ Jesus for you. (1 Thess. 5:18)

Day 5: Focus! Focus! Focus!

It is easy to become totally focused on a child, on the situation at hand, or on what is *not* happening! Peter became wrongly focused after joining Christ for a walk on the water, didn't he (Matt. 14:30)? When Peter stepped out of the boat, he was completely secure walking on the water as long as he was gazing at Jesus. As soon as his focus shifted to himself and his circumstances, though, he sank. How great that Peter got out of the boat in the first place (he was the only one who did). But the same will happen to us if we shift our focus from God.

If we turn all our time and attention to the salvation of our children or on what they are doing, we will start to despair. This happens because we're focused on circumstances we can't control (and often on ourselves), instead of focusing on Jesus and trusting him to do what is best. When we are in this state, we will also fail to love God and others (including the wayward child) the way we should. Also consider the fact that Satan is crouching at the door to use your trial for evil—but don't let him! (1 Peter 5:8).

Instead, pray for perspective and work to maintain it. *Set your affections and hopes on Jesus where they belong* (Phil. 1:21). Ask yourself whether your children and their salvation mean more to you than Christ (i.e., idolatry). Rehearse that there is more to life than *just* the state of your children. There is the love and faithfulness of God to you. There are other

177

blessings. There are other needs. Don't be consumed with your children and their spiritual condition and choices. The salvation of a child is one of the greatest desires/burdens we as parents have, but it should not be what we live for. Only God, if he wills, can make this happen.

Confess, if need be, any idolatry. Pray regularly for your child and be available for God to use you, but move on and focus on serving God's kingdom. Engage in other prayers, ministries, and activities, even if it is difficult at first. There *is* more to life!

> So whether we are at home or away, *we make it our aim to please him.* (2 Cor. 5:9, emphasis added)

> When Christ *who is your life* appears, then you also will appear with him in glory. (Col. 3:4, emphasis added)

Day 6: Are you with the program?

Our overall perspective has a lot to do with how we handle trials that involve other people. We must not just *cope* with the situation we are facing nor reluctantly *accept* the situation, but rather *embrace* the situation as being God's best for us at this time (2 Cor. 12:7–10). If God is testing you through your children, realize that this, at least for the moment, is his perfect and all-wise plan for you. Humbly allow God to reveal what you *really* believe and to show you areas where you are not strong or like Jesus.

If you are humble and trusting before the Lord, he will use this difficult time to strengthen your walk with him and remove the dross of sin from your life. Instead of leaving you where you are, God loves you enough to mold you into the image of his Son.

> It is good for me that I was afflicted, that I might learn your statutes. . . . I know, O LORD, that your rules are righteous, and that in faithfulness you have afflicted me. Let your steadfast love comfort me according to your promise to your servant. (Ps. 119:71–76, selected portions)

This trial is perfectly designed for what needs to be accomplished in you and for you. In the midst of what seems like a completely negative circumstance, God can be glorified as you are changed more and more into the image of his Son.

> And we know that for those who love God all things work together for good, for those who are called according to his purpose. For those whom he foreknew he also predestined to be *conformed to the image of his Son*, in order that he might be the firstborn among many brothers. (Rom. 8:28–29, emphasis added)

Day 7: Fight bitterness! Not God!

If we are not thankful in all our circumstances, often what creeps in is bitterness. This can be directed at a rebellious child or even at God. Bitterness happens when we think we've been wronged (whether this is true or not), become angry, and cease loving. Nursing anger results in an abiding resentment, which leads to more sin.

> Let all bitterness and wrath and anger and clamor and slander be put away from you, along with all malice. Be kind to one another, tenderhearted, forgiving one another, as God in Christ forgave you. (Eph. 4:31–32)

Instead of being angry and bitter, we are to trust and be kind, compassionate, and forgiving. We are to go the extra mile (Matt. 5:41), return good for evil (Rom. 12:21), and pray for those who persecute us (Matt. 5:44). If we do not obey these commands we may find ourselves doing ridiculous things such as sharing the gospel in anger or using anger to try to change the heart.

> For the anger of man does not produce the righteousness that God requires. (James 1:20)

Bitterness can be hard to see in ourselves because we're so busy rehearsing the reasons why we didn't deserve what has happened to us. Ask yourself these questions to help evaluate whether you're bitter:

- Am I withdrawing my love and commitment to my child or God?
- Am I shocked and appalled that my child would sin against *me*?
- Do I wonder how God could do/allow this to happen to *me*?
- Am I not willing (or finding it very difficult) to do good to my child or for God?
- Do I feel I deserve to be treated better by God?
- Do I find myself avoiding my child?
- Do I secretly delight in his misfortune?

180

- Do I see his sin as the "log" and mine as the "speck" before God?

Repent of any bitterness that you have! Make glorifying God your focus instead of dwelling on how you're being treated.

Day 8: God understands!

God the Father discloses to us on the pages of Scripture what he went through with unbelieving Israel for over five hundred years. As a parent, he knows what you are going through. He has been there.

> Hear, O heavens, and give ear, O earth; for the Lord has spoken: "Children have I reared and brought up, but they have rebelled against me. . . . They have forsaken the Lord, they have despised the Holy One of Israel, they are utterly estranged." (Isa. 1:2–4)

He knows what it is to be rejected by those whom he has loved and cared for. He knows what it is like to see a loved one headed for disaster. He knows what it is to long for his children to return to their senses (Matt. 23:37). He knows what it is to have anguish over his own, although they may cause it.

> "In all their affliction he was afflicted . . . ." (Isa. 63:9)

You can be assured that God the Father is able to sympathize with you and knows how to work with the wayward. Jesus, our High Priest, understands when we grow weary. Hebrews 4:15–16 tells us to whom and where we can go when we are weak and tempted.

> For we do not have a high priest who is unable to sympathize with our weaknesses, but one who in every respect has been tempted as we are, yet without sin. Let us then with confidence draw near to the *throne of grace*, that we may receive mercy and find grace to help in time of need. (emphasis added)

Our High Priest sympathizes with us because he, too, has been tempted in all things—yet without sinning. This should give us great confidence to approach his *throne of grace* looking for mercy! Charles Spurgeon says, "Lest the glow and brilliance of the word *throne* should be too much for mortal vision, our text . . . [also] presents us with the soft, gentle radiance of that delightful word *grace*."[1]

Day 9: Is God's grace enough?

It is crucial to trust that Christ's grace is *really* sufficient for what you need, no matter what happens! Do you trust him in this way? If you humbly depend on his grace, it *will* be there. Unfortunately, in the English language, we have come to use *sufficient* to mean less than perfect. We might say, "That car is sufficient." But we don't mean it's superior. We mean it'll do or it'll get me where I need to go, but it's not

---

1. C. H. Spurgeon, "The Throne of Grace," sermon preached at the Metropolitan Tabernacle, Newington, London, Nov. 19, 1871.

great! When Paul uses the word *sufficient,* it does not carry a negative meaning at all. It means all you could ever need or want . . . and more.

> But he [Jesus Christ] said to me [the apostle Paul], "*My grace is sufficient* for you, for my power is made perfect in weakness." (2 Cor. 12:9, adaptation added)

If we don't believe that God's grace is more than sufficient and better than anything else, we will turn to "false refuges" for relief, rather than to God for grace. Because of emotional pain, you may think it better to distract yourselves with television or business. You may be tempted to bring relief through self-medication, but the Lord can give *sufficient* grace and comfort through his Word and prayer. Acting on the desire to escape reality, or to forget it, will not get you anywhere. It will only leave you further discouraged in the end. More importantly, it will not bring God glory or give him the opportunity to be God to you.

Day 10: Humility vs. pride! And the winner is?

Humility is the mind-set of Christ (Phil. 2:5–8), while pride is the prevailing attitude of the evil one (Isa. 14:12–15) and us when we are responding in the flesh (Gal. 5:15–17). Humility is focused on God and others, while pride is self-focused (Phil. 2:3–5). You can be sure that Satan wants to use this situation in your family to promote pride in your life. There are many ways in which you may be tempted to respond in pride.

Prideful Response	Verse	Humble Response
Trying to cope and go on in your own strength (no prayer for God's grace and you *only* want the trial removed for your benefit).	Three times I pleaded with the Lord about this, that it should leave me. But he said to me, "My grace is sufficient for you, for my power is made perfect in weakness." Therefore I will boast all the more gladly of my weaknesses, so that the power of Christ may rest upon me. (2 Cor. 12:8–9) Let us then with confidence draw near to the throne of grace, that we may receive mercy and find grace to help in time of need. (Heb. 4:16)	Being dependent on God in prayer and trusting in his strength. Understanding that your strength is God's rival and your weakness his instrument.
Dwelling on or acting out what others might think.	For am I now seeking the approval of man, or of God? Or am I trying to please man? If I were still trying to please man, I would not be a servant of Christ. (Gal. 1:10)	Seek to please God alone and be satisfied with his love, commitment, and opinion.
Being defensive or defending your parenting.	But with me it is a very small thing that I should be judged by you or by any human court. In fact, I do not even judge myself. For I am not aware of anything against myself, but I am not thereby acquitted. It is the Lord who judges me. Therefore do not pronounce judgment before the time, before the Lord comes, who will bring to light the things now hidden in darkness and will disclose the purposes of the heart. (1 Cor. 4:3–5)	Readily admit that you are not perfect and seek to be a better parent with God's help.
Believing or acting like you are flawless in your parenting.	"Give, I pray thee, glory to the Lord God of Israel, and make confession unto him; and tell me what thou hast done; hide it not from me." (Josh. 7:19, KJV)	Confess your sins to God and to your son or daughter.

184

Prideful Response	Verse	Humble Response
Thinking that you would do things differently if you were God.	"For as the heavens are higher than the earth, so are my ways higher than your ways and my thoughts than your thoughts." (Isa. 55:9) Therefore let those who suffer according to God's will entrust their souls to a faithful Creator while doing good. (1 Peter 4:19)	Confess to God that he is good and all-wise, and sees how all things work together—and you do not.
Being disgusted with your son or daughter as if you are better than they.	For who sees anything different in you? What do you have that you did not receive? If then you received it, why do you boast as if you did not receive it? (1 Cor. 4:7)	See your sin as no better before God and that it is only by his grace that you do not do the same or worse!
Focusing more on what is happening to you than the needs of your child, what God wants of you, or God's glory in the situation.	In humility count others more significant than yourselves. Let each of you look not only to his own interests, but also to the interests of others. (Phil. 2:3–4)	Focusing on how God wants you to respond for his glory and for the needs of your child.
Thinking that you have the power (or responsibility) to save your children or the power to keep them from being saved.	Behold, the Lord's hand is not shortened, that it cannot save. . . . (Isa. 59:1) "No one can come to me unless the Father who sent me draws him. And I will raise him up on the last day." (John 6:44)	Seek to be a faithful parent in the ways that God has said and entrust your child's heart and salvation to him.

Day 11: The comparison trap

It is another manifestation of pride to compare your family or your parenting with those of others! Sometimes we compare ourselves with others with painful envy because we believe we should have what *they* have. We are comparing ourselves in self-pity (putting God on the witness stand) or in self-judgment (putting ourselves on the witness stand). Both are an unprofitable *self-focus*. Examining our parenting for faithfulness and needed repentance is a good thing, but making wishful comparisons and examining outcomes in order to place blame is not. Take those thoughts captive!

There will be times when you see evidence of good parenting and young people who are doing well and serving the Lord. The Lord wants you to respond with thankfulness. However, it is important to know that when you think you see the perfect, euphoric family, you don't! No family is perfect or perfectly happy. All homes have their challenges and sins. All people have trials in their lives even if their children are not currently a significant one. Lasting euphoria is in heaven alone—which our difficulties should help us long for.

At other times we compare ourselves in order to pat ourselves on the back or make us feel better. Although we can take note of other parents and their families to learn from them, we dare not measure ourselves by them or them by us. We must measure *ourselves* by God, but with humility, grace, and hope. Humble parents of godly children will tell you that God has worked *in spite of* their parenting skills!

It is also prideful to measure other parents or children by a snapshot of sinful or selfish behavior. Be careful when you don't know the whole story. In other words, refrain from comparison and judgments, especially from a distance! If God has not placed you in a position to be fully in the know and to be of help, believe the best and remember it is the Lord's responsibility to reveal the truth when he comes back (1 Cor. 4:5). In the meantime, be a faithful parent and don't compare yourself with other parents whether they are good or bad.

> Not that we dare to classify or compare ourselves with some of those who are commending themselves. But when they measure themselves by one another and compare themselves with one another, they are without understanding. (2 Cor. 10:12)

Day 12: Keep short accounts

It is important to see your sin for what it is, without excuse. Although it is easy to shift blame when someone else is not doing as he should, resist the temptation. Be sure to confess your sins against God and your unbelieving child as you walk this path. Be specific and willing to share your plan of how you will repent (change).

Be humble enough to deal with your own wrongdoing. How ironic to be upset with our children because they won't humble themselves before God, while we refuse to humble ourselves in confession before him and them. What a mixed message!

Confession is often a catalyst for trust and bringing down walls with a son or daughter. Other fruits of confession with repentance are peace, joy, and the respect of others. Most importantly, confession (and moving on to change) is what glorifies God when you have messed up.

> Then Joshua said to Achan, "My son, give glory to the LORD God of Israel . . . tell me now what you have done; do not hide it from me." (Josh. 7:19)

> If we confess our sins, he is faithful and just to forgive us our sins and to cleanse us from all unrighteousness. (1 John 1:9)

Day 13: Are you "keeping" your heart?

Another area of paramount importance for you as a parent is to renew or change your confused, anxious, erroneous, and/or sinful thoughts. Are you keeping your *heart* where it should be (Heb. 4:12; Luke 5:22)? If you are not taking thoughts captive and speaking the truth to your own heart while in this trial, you will surely spiral down into despair and sin, becoming a poor testimony to your child and others. *What if?* can turn into *I know*, and soon you are gripped with anxiety and fear. Some thoughts may be true but are void of God or his promises. This makes them unprofitable, hopeless, and therefore sinful thoughts. On the other hand, a God-filled, hopeful, thankful, or trusting thought can make all the difference in the world. Following the pattern of Philippians 4:7–9 to pray, put on God's kind of thought, and do what is right will mean the difference between victory and defeat. Here are some examples of thoughts that need renewing.

Wrong Thought	Verse	Right Thought	Right Action
My son is foolish, lost, and headed for destruction.	Isaiah 59:1; Jeremiah 32:27	My son is lost right now, but Lord, you are able to save. I thank you that the most hardened heart can be changed in an instant.	Pray for God to work for your son's salvation. Prepare to be a good witness as God gives you opportunity.
What if they don't ever come to Christ? I couldn't bear it.	Hebrews 4:16; Psalm 139:10	Lord, I thank you that you will help me with whatever happens. I also thank you that the story is not over yet.	Pray for your own witness and others' witness in their life. Study God's faithfulness to sustain.
What if they do something really foolish, bringing more detriment to themselves, more heartache, and more reproach?	Genesis 50:20; 1 Peter 4:12–19	I thank you Lord that you are in control, that you promise to give grace for whatever happens, and that you are able to use anything for your glory and the good of all concerned (including other believers). I thank you that the situation is not any worse and that you are able to restrain them.	Pray for and trust God's all-wise restraint on their lives. Focus on using the situation for God's glory and pleasing him, not on what others think.

Wrong Thought	Verse	Right Thought	Right Action
This isn't fair! How could you not save them, Lord, after my trust in you and all I have done for you and them?	Deuteronomy 32:4; Psalm 92:15	My faithful Lord who died for me, I thank you that you know why this is happening and that there is no unrighteousness in you at all. You always do what is right. You are not obligated to save anyone, and yet you do. What I deserve is hell, and so do they, but you are a gracious God.	Pray for God's mercy even though it is undeserved. Continue serving God because he deserves it and you trust who he is.
Enough is enough! I can't take this anymore.	1 Corinthians 10:13; 2 Corinthians 12:9–10; 2 Corinthians 9:8; Job 41:11	I thank you, Lord, that you promise you will never give me more than I can handle with your help. I thank you that you are with me and that your grace is more than sufficient. You are in this to be God to me, make me like you, and glorify yourself. I can do all things with your help.	Pray for God's grace and trust him for it. Allow the body of Christ to be part of what is going on as others pray for and assist you. Think how you can turn your focus to others and serving God for his glory.

Wrong Thought	Verse	Right Thought	Right Action
What if they are in danger?	Psalm 145:5; Matthew 6:34	Lord, I praise you that you are in control of the situation. I thank you that, as far as I know, they are okay (or you can use anything in their lives for salvation and for good).	Pray for God's protection and grace, as well as knowledge of the danger, if the Lord believes you need it. Then, turn your focus to serving others and God's kingdom.
I don't know what to do or how to help them.	Job 12:16; Psalm 147:5	Lord, I thank you that you know all things, that you know what is needed and are able to accomplish it.	Get counsel on what God would have you do, if anything. Then, give them and their situation over to an all-wise and all-powerful God. Be patient and endure with his help.

When in an extreme trial, our thoughts (and therefore emotions) can be all over the map. What is more important than the *types* of thoughts that come to mind is what you do with them. As Martin Luther said, "You can't stop the birds from flying around your head but you can keep them from nesting in your hair." Are you willing to "love the Lord your God . . . with all your mind" (Mark 12:30) and "direct your heart in the way" (Prov. 23:19)? In Appendix D you will find a worksheet to assist you with new thoughts.

> Keep your heart with all vigilance, for from it flow the springs
> of life. (Prov. 4:23)

Day 14: Their unbelief is not your fault

The accusation (by you, Satan, or others) that you are responsible for your child's unbelief must be rejected with truth. What you have or haven't done probably has influenced them, but it does *not* keep them from believing or *make* them rebel. Contrary to popular opinion, none of us are excused or determined by our environment or past. We all have a choice in our responses to what happens around us, and God will hold each person responsible (Rom. 14:11–12). Remember that God (who is perfect) parented Israel and yet they rebelled (Isa. 1:2–4). Our children are responsible for their own sin. Of course, if there is sin in your life that has encouraged your children on their *own* wayward path, repent. Still, whether or not your child is saved is a matter between God and them—not based on what you do or don't do (John 6:44).

> The soul who sins shall die. The son shall not suffer for the iniquity
> of the father, nor the father suffer for the iniquity of the son. The
> righteousness of the righteous shall be upon himself, and the
> wickedness of the wicked shall be upon himself. (Ezek. 18:20)

Day 15: No retreat—no withdrawal

As Christians we don't have the option of quitting or withdrawing from what God has called us to do. God has given us the job of parenting these precious children! We are to love God and them, no matter what. Our job description certainly

192

changes over the years, but resigning is not an option. Galatians 6:9 says, "And let us *not grow weary* of doing good, for in due season we will reap, if we do not give up" (emphasis added). We must be *steadfast* in our commitment to God's glory and to doing good to our children. Pray for God's help in this.

Since God never gives us more than we can bear, we know that we can *continue on* in well-doing, or God would make a way of escape. Remember the old saying, "Two wrongs don't make a right"? Well, that is true here. If your child isn't following the Lord, your falling away, giving up in frustration, or contemplating throwing in the towel would only make things twice as wrong! Strive instead to be a *constant example of faithfulness* to your child. Your love for God and your child should be far greater than anything your child has done or God has allowed.

When we contemplate giving up, it is a sure sign that we were parenting or serving God for the wrong reason(s). If you find yourself in bitter retreat, it is time to remember God's faithfulness (in spite of you) and why we serve him. We serve him out of gratitude for his undeserved love and mercy toward us, and because it brings him the glory he deserves.

> Therefore since we receive a kingdom which cannot be shaken, let us *show gratitude*, by which *we may offer* to God an acceptable service with reverence and awe . . . . (Heb. 12:28, NASB, emphasis added)

Day 16: Resist isolation

Christians are never encouraged to live their own lives separated from other believers. It is easy to withdraw from the body of Christ if you are struggling with a trial. This may be because of the fear of man or because you don't want to address sin and change. Both are prideful. Fear comes into play because you don't want to admit that you struggle or face what people may think of your trial. Some believers may be judgmental or jump to conclusions, but withdrawing from the body of Christ to avoid them is wrong and detrimental to all those involved.

Talk with your pastor and a few good friends for prayer, encouragement, and counsel on what to do in parenting situations. Godly older men and women, especially ones who have weathered storms, can be a wealth of wisdom for you. Utilize your family of God. Galatians 6:2 tells us to "bear one another's burdens." People can't help you bear up under a trial if they don't know what you are going through!

When sharing with others, be careful not to gossip about or slander your children. Be discerning about when it's appropriate to share prayer requests and how many details to broadcast. Keep in mind that your son or daughter can change but a reputation is sometimes hard to restore.

If you have friends who don't understand what you're going through and are not helpful, don't become bitter or frustrated with them. Our trials are uniquely tailored to suit us as individuals. Sometimes our friends may not completely understand until they've faced a similar hardship. Sometimes they don't have enough information. Don't hold this against them, and remember that God understands everything!

> Whoever isolates himself seeks his own desire; he breaks out against all sound judgment. (Prov. 18:1)

Day 17: The story is not over

Be assured that God is able to save them in his perfect time and his perfect way.

Behold, the LORD's hand is not shortened, that it cannot save,
or his ear dull, that it cannot hear . . . . (Isa. 59:1)

Pray for your son or daughter without ceasing. George Müller, an English evangelist and philanthropist in the 1800s, prayed for three of his dear friends' salvation for years. Reportedly, two of them came to Christ during his lifetime, but the third one didn't. In God's goodness, this third friend was saved at Müller's funeral!

Resist the temptation to worry about the future. Instead, thank God for his longsuffering and his mercy. Many great saints were saved late in life and gave testimony of a parent or grandparent who faithfully prayed for them for years. It is never right to give up on our children or on God's grace and ability to work.

Day 18: It's still just a speck

Even if this difficult time persists and seems like forever, it is only a speck in light of eternity.

For it is all for your sake, so that as grace extends to more and more people it may increase thanksgiving, to the glory of God. So we do not lose heart. Though our outer nature is wasting away, our inner nature is being renewed day by day. *For this slight momentary affliction is preparing for us an eternal weight of glory beyond all comparison,* as we look not to the things

195

that are seen but to the things that are unseen. For the things that are seen are transient, but *the things that are unseen are eternal.* (2 Cor. 4:15–18, emphasis added)

As you look at your life here, see it as a dot and picture eternity as a never-ending line. Our time here counts, but it is *momentary* compared with eternity. In the midst of our trials, remember that one day we will be with our Lord and there will be no more tears. This should be our ultimate hope and expectation. We should be "waiting for our blessed hope, the appearing of the glory of our great God and Savior Jesus Christ" (Titus 2:13).

Day 19: Your *own* responses are most important

You will do far better for God and all concerned if you focus *more* on your own responses than what your son or daughter is doing or not doing. God is not pleased when we focus on another's sin and make excuse for our own.

"Why do you see the speck that is in your brother's eye, but do not notice the log that is in your own eye? Or how can you say to your brother, 'Let me take the speck out of your eye,' when there is the log in your own eye? You hypocrite, first take the log out of your own eye, and then you will see clearly to take the speck out of your brother's eye." (Matt. 7:3–5)

It is easy to become caught up in what others are doing wrong and forget to see what God is trying to do in us. Don't act like Moses sometimes did when the children of Israel sinned. There were occasions when he became angry at God's people and even angry at God (Ex. 32:19; Num. 11:10–12). Instead, we need to revere God

196

and his commands for us even when our children do wrong. We must focus on *us*—not dwell on our children's disobedience and how we've been offended. For you, God is *most* concerned about your responses and your heart being matured into the image of his Son. We can't control our circumstances, but by God's grace and for God's glory we can control our responses to them.

> Let the words of my mouth and the meditation of my heart be acceptable in your sight, O LORD, my rock and my redeemer. (Ps. 19:14)

Day 20: Remember how dear and amazing your children are!

If your young persons have grown more challenging and sinful, their behavior can begin to cloud your perspective. They are still God's creation and they are still *your* precious children (Ps. 139:13). As deficient as their love may be at times, deep in their hearts they have a natural love for you, their parent(s). Remember that one day they will likely remember your love for them and that they love you too! When times are tough, go back to fond memories of your children—remember how much joy they have brought and can again if God so wills. Don't let the few snapshots of present difficulties cancel out the movie-strip of many times of joy—certainly not your love.

Remind yourself that your children are *still* gifted in their own ways and are not as bad as they could be, thanks to God's common goodness. Think of things about them that you love or have loved for which you can be thankful. It would be good to add this to your Gratitude List from Day 6.

197

Finally, remember that a wayward young person is *still* one of God's gifts to you. God provides his gifts to both bless us and sanctify us. Surely your son or daughter has brought blessing, and God is using them to sanctify you in a great way now. You must thank him for giving you the perfect *gift* (child) for you.

> Behold, children are a heritage from the Lord, the fruit of the womb a reward. (Ps. 127:3)

Day 21: Be an encourager whenever you can

Don't just see the areas that need to be corrected with your child, but also encourage them. Love them for who they are (God's unique creation and your children) and encourage them, even though they are unsaved. It will go a long way in your relationship if you are like the Lord was to the churches (Rev. 2–3). He dealt with their sin and shortcomings, but he capitalized on encouraging them first. Within bounds, it's probably a good rule of thumb to *encourage them all the more* when contention abounds.

Think purposefully about your children's natural abilities. Maybe they are gifted athletically, good students, or musically talented. Do they have a soft heart for a little brother or are they a loyal friend? Whatever it is, even if it's small, find a way to compliment and encourage them. Work to break the vicious cycle of negative behavior and your negative perspective. Strive to draw them in by more of a Barnabas personality, encouraging them in both word and deed.

> Thus Joseph, who was also called by the apostles Barnabas (which means son of encouragement) . . . sold a field that belonged to him and brought the money and laid it at the apostles' feet. (Acts 4:36–37)

Day 22: Distance is dangerous

Although the natural reaction to difference and difficulty is distance, you need to work against detachment and be involved in the children's world. Take an active interest in what your child likes or create something of interest to both of you. It is important to do what you can to cultivate something that brings you together, since the spiritual does not. Keep in mind that "we ourselves were once foolish, disobedient, led astray, slaves to various passions and pleasures . . ." (Titus 3:3). You must endure any hardships and pursue them, even if they act like they want to be left alone. They don't *really*; not when it comes to your positive involvement.

> [The Lord Jesus said to the church at Ephesus,] "I know your words, your toil and your patient endurance, and how you cannot bear with those who are evil, but have tested those who call themselves apostles and are not, and found them to be false. I know you are enduring patiently and bearing up for my name's sake, and you have not grown weary." (Rev. 2:2–3, adaptation added)

Distance is dangerous to your relationship and your witness. If you are not intentional about creating some bridges and fun, it will not be long until all your dealings with your wandering young person are negative. Enjoy baking, shopping, camping, or reading with them. Learn how to play their favorite game. Cheer for the same college or professional sports team. Ride bikes or take up jogging. Make extraordinary effort to go to their games, concerts, or plays. Find something they enjoy (that won't make you compromise your walk with the Lord) and take the initiative to wholeheartedly join them. Enter into their world!

Day 23: What is your expectation?

Don't be caught off guard when unbelievers act like unbelievers. It's likely that you will see selfishness and hurtfulness as well as instability in your unsaved child. As a son or daughter continues on the path of unbelief, this fruit may become more drastic. They ultimately do not have the ability to live for anything but their own advantage. It's only a believer whom "the love of Christ controls . . .[so that they] no longer live for themselves but for him who for their sake died and was raised" (2 Cor. 5:14–15; adaptation added).

> But understand this, that in the last days there will come times of difficulty. For people will be lovers of self, lovers of money, proud, arrogant, abusive, disobedient to their parents, ungrateful, unholy, heartless, unappeasable, slanderous, without self-control, brutal, not loving good, treacherous, reckless, swollen with conceit, lovers of pleasure rather than lovers of God, having the appearance of godliness, but denying its power. (2 Tim. 3:1–5)

When you see behavior you never dreamed of, give thanks to God that things are not as bad as they could be. Without ignoring wrong behavior or poor choices, accept who they really are. If you are not realistic about their state, you will most likely sin in your response or dip into despair. Remember also that their selfishness and instability can show them their need for Christ.

Day 24: It's not about you!

Remember, it's not all about *you* and what you are going through! It may be harder to honor God and return love to a child who is being selfish and mean, but the fact is that Christ was faithful and loved you when you were his enemy (Rom. 5:8). It's important not to take their lack of love, meanness, or rebellion so personally. This will only add to the wall they are building, and you will regret it. Know that when your children are angry at your reasonable authority, they really are angry at God's authority.

> And the Lord said to Samuel, "Obey the voice of the people in all that they say to you, for they have not rejected you, but they have rejected me from being king over them." (1 Sam. 8:7)

Be on guard against (and perhaps repent of) becoming self-focused. When you are self-focused, you are not loving God or your child as you should. This situation is an opportunity for the gospel and to put on love (Phil. 2:14–15). Trust that there really is some love underneath all their sin, and a good purpose in what God is allowing. Your focus should not be you, your trial, or your feelings, but God's kingdom and your child's need for Christ.

201

Day 25: Anger is not righteous or profitable

Repent of any anger you have against your unbelieving child for not believing and/or for the result of being foolish at times. Because the faith to repent and believe is a gift from God, you should still have compassion on them. You must not excuse any manifestations of your own sinful anger. At the base of your anger is pride. But for the grace of God, there you go also (1 Cor. 4:7). Ask God to help you deal with your pride and angry reaction to their rejection of Christ. Remember, "The anger of man does not produce the righteousness that God requires" (James 1:20).

> Let all bitterness and wrath and anger and clamor and slander be put away from you, along with all malice. Be kind to one another, tenderhearted, forgiving one another, as God in Christ forgave you. (Eph. 4:31–32)

My Sinful Response	My Righteous Response
Anger	Go to God with my hurt, knowing that the greatest offense of your child is against God. 1 Peter 4:19
Disgust	Understand they have a heart of stone just like you once did. and you are not better than they. 1 Corinthians 4:7; Ezekiel 36:26
Pull away	Draw near in sacrificial love and care. Romans 12:9–21
In anger give the gospel	Gently point them to their greatest need. 2 Corinthians 5:13–21
Physically hit or push them	Firmly minister consequences. Ephesians 4:31
Preach at them	Instruct them in little segments in a humble and loving way. Deuteronomy 6:6–9
Focus on their sin instead of yours	Humble yourself and confess your sins to God and to your child. Matthew 7:1–5

Day 26: Don't be a man-pleaser

Fight the temptation to be afraid of your son or daughter's reactions and shrink back from what you know is right. As we seek to do the right thing and exercise the truth in love, we must leave the outcome to God (Rom. 8:28). You must be faithful to do what is best for your child.

> So then, as we have opportunity, let us do good to *everyone* . . . ."
> (Gal. 6:10, emphasis added)

This can be hard, especially when the right thing may mean an extreme result. We must love our son or daughter enough to endure their temporary unhappiness, scorn, and perhaps rejection. You may need to confront their sin, turn them in to the police, or force help on them for drug or alcohol abuse. No one will appreciate these things at the time, but that shouldn't stop you from trying to do what is necessary to please God and help them.

> For am I now seeking the approval of man, or of God? Or am I trying to please man? If I were still trying to please man, I would not be a servant of Christ. (Gal. 1:10)

Day 27: Analyze your prayers for your children

One of the best things you can do for your children is to pray for them and your relationship with them. Pray instead of worry. Pray alone. Pray with your spouse. Pray with others in your church family. Persevere in prayer, even if it seems nothing is happening. It is important to pray biblically, according to God's will and not just about your own desires.

Analyze whether or not your prayers for your child are in line with God's truth, for his glory, and for your child's greatest good. Biblical prayers would be:

- For God to have mercy and save them for his glory and their good (Ps. 116:5; Rom. 9:14–16; 10:1; Eph. 2:4–5).
- For his perfect timing (Deut. 32:4; Ps. 31:15).
- For God in his common grace to protect them from the evil one's schemes, evil people, themselves, and harm (Ps. 103:19; 146:9).
- For God to help you (and give clear opportunities) to be the light and witness you should be (Phil. 4:9; Col. 4:3).
- For their eyes to be opened to the world's futility and the destructiveness of sin (James 4:4–5; 1 John 2:15–17).
- That your love and commitment to them would be clear to them, and for opportunities to express both (Eph. 5:1).

Analyze *when* you pray and the *result* of your prayers. Do your prayers quickly turn to ones that are thankful, hopeful, and trusting? Be careful that you are not just rehearsing how bad the situation is. Instead, rehearse biblical requests along with who God is and his promises. Are *you* worse off after prayer, or does it refocus you on your wonderful Lord and his kingdom?

Continue steadfastly in prayer, being watchful in it with thanksgiving. (Col. 4:2)

Do not be anxious about anything, but in everything by prayer and supplication with thanksgiving let your requests be made known to God. (Phil. 4:6)

Day 28: Be a smiling tank!

Be lovingly firm but also immovable on basic limits and house rules. These will be nonnegotiable. Because you are responsible to God for what goes on in your home, you must never allow anything immoral, anything unlawful, or anything or anyone dangerous in your home. Guard against the extremes of either letting wrong things slide or acting like the Gestapo! In a godly way, you should require a level of responsibility and respect in the home or all chaos ensues. It is sin on your part *not* to deal with issues and take the proper action (Titus 1:6).

On the other hand, be aware that some things are not hills to die on, especially when you are dealing with an unbelieving teenager. Great discernment is needed here to differentiate between the "camel" (big) issues and the "gnat" (sideline) issues (Matt. 23:24). Sometimes we can magnify the minors and miss the majors.

The influence of a rebellious older teen is cause for careful consideration and action. The unbelieving child must be willing to cooperate with the parents concerning his or her influence on younger siblings. Although it is difficult (and a last resort), there are times that the right and loving thing to do (for all concerned) is to help the unsaved teen find another place to live. Preferably this would be a place that offers biblical counsel and redirection, if they are willing.

The book *When Good Kids Make Bad Choices* can be very helpful for parents of rebellious teens.[2] Whatever the issue or the action needed, ask God for the grace to deal with it his way and with unwavering love for him and your child.

> Therefore, my beloved brothers, be steadfast, immovable, always abounding in the work of the Lord, knowing that in the Lord your labor is not in vain. (1 Cor. 15:58)

Day 29: Deal with one thing at a time

You may notice a tendency to lose focus when your children make a very sinful or foolish choice. It is important to address only one issue at a time. It can be tempting to throw everything negative about their lives or their whole times of waywardness at them. This is more than likely evidence of bitterness. In our frustration and desperation to help them "see the light," it is easy to remind them of every thing they've ever done wrong—all in one five-minute lecture! If you do, they will no doubt miss anything true you are saying and reject your counsel on the matter at hand. Refrain from bringing up their unsaved state every time you speak with them about an issue. Just stick to the matter at hand and deal with it without exaggerating. Be sure to gather all the data before addressing what seems to be true. It will be easy to assume the worst in light of their history, but don't do it.

> A word fitly spoken is like apples of gold in a setting of silver. (Prov. 25:11)

2. Elyse Fitzpatrick, Jim Newheiser, and Laura Hendrickson, *When Good Kids Make Bad Choices* (Eugene, OR: Harvest House, 2005).

Day 30: Grace, marvelous grace

Grace is the undeserved help of God, which he loves to give to the humble of heart—those who know that they are undeserving, that he is always right, and that God deserves all (James 4:6). In the same way that God's unmerited help for our salvation is only given to those who see their need for Jesus, we must also see our *daily* need before we will "be strengthened by the grace that is in Christ Jesus" (2 Tim. 2:1). It is the supernatural power of God that will help you to endure and honor him. Grace is the encouragement and assistance of God himself toward you. It may come in the form of his comfort, his strength, his peace, his wisdom, or his gift of faith. Giving his marvelous grace is a major way the Lord cares for us and shows us he is our personal God.

> For he is our God, and we are the people of his pasture, and the sheep of his hand. (Ps. 95:7)

Through the grace of God, we come to know him and his attributes in a more intimate way. We can personally experience his faithfulness and power. It is a glorious, incomparable thing to see God's personal hand in our lives. Experiencing the grace of God is the *only* thing that can cause believers to say with Paul:

> Therefore I will boast all the more gladly of my weaknesses, so that the power of Christ may rest upon me. For the sake of Christ, then, I am content with weaknesses, insults, hardships, persecutions, and calamities. For when I am weak, then I am strong. (2 Cor. 12:9–10)

Conclusion

As you end this month of devotions for difficult times, we hope God's Word and principles have encouraged you, renewed your perspective, and helped set your direction. If not, it's time to "take another lap around Mount Sinai" and do the whole thirty days again. I, Stuart, know this as an experienced lap runner! Reviewing these truths is a must for any of us on the parenting journey. As you, the parent of a wandering child, make your way through what seems like the wilderness, remember that *you* are in process, *your child* is in process, and *your God* is faithful and can help you to be a more faithful parent in any and every situation.

11

Conclusion

N ext to our salvation and our spouses, our children are the most important gift that God has given us. What love and joy they bring into our lives and, at times, what great sorrow! We love them. We sacrifice for them. We rightly long for them to do well in life and to love the Lord with all their hearts. We desire for them to be wise and not foolish. We want them to fear God and submit to his authority.

Young parents wake up to a new adventure every day. They often call older, more experienced parents for advice. Martha's pastor and his wife, John and Lynn Crotts, did this when their first child, Charissa, learned to pull up and stand clinging to the side of the crib. The problem was that she could not get back down! When they laid her back down, she popped right back up. The battle of wills began in earnest. So, John and Lynn called some friends who were more experienced. What they learned was that there is no "the" way to deal with such antics but there are several common-sense "a" ways. John and Lynn could no more guarantee that Charissa would stay put than they could guarantee she would be saved.

Like all Christian parents, though, John and Lynn *can* be guaranteed (by their own choice) to be *faithful to God's Word by his grace and for his glory.* One of the recurring themes throughout this book is that only God can save a child if he so wills. Salvation *is* a one-hundred percent work of God. So teach your children about God and about our Lord Jesus Christ and his work on the cross. Don't be one of those "provoking parents" but instead "bring them up in the discipline and instruction of the Lord" (Eph. 6:4). Fix your hope on Christ and look forward to how God is going to work sovereignly in your life and the lives of your children.

As a faithful parent, continue to grow in God's grace and take delight in his commands. Let your children see that God's commands are your joy and not a burden. No matter the ages of your children, love and enjoy them. Show love by being patient and kind. Be fully convinced of God's goodness. Last, but certainly not least, pray. Base your prayers on God's Word, acknowledging what you know to be true of the Lord. Come often and boldly to the "throne of grace, that [you] may receive mercy and find grace to help in time of need" (Heb. 4:16).

We could think of no better way to end *The Faithful Parent* than with a prayer that you can pray or adapt for your use when you pray for your children. Pray it thoughtfully and earnestly, meditating on the accompanying Scripture. Make your humble requests to God and wait patiently for his answer.

The Prayer	Scriptural Basis
Heavenly Father, I acknowledge and praise you for who you are.	"Pray then like this: 'Our Father in heaven, hallowed be your name.'" (Matt. 6:9)
Thank you for the blessing of our children.	"Behold, children are a heritage from the LORD, the fruit of the womb a reward." (Ps. 127:3) " . . . give thanks in all circumstances; for this is the will of God in Christ Jesus for you." (1 Thess. 5:18) "Do not be anxious about anything, but in everything by prayer and supplication *with thanksgiving* let your requests be made known to God." (Phil. 4:6, emphasis added)
Thank you that you have given us our children to love them and *so that we can learn to love you more . . .*	"'Teacher, which is the great commandment in the Law?' And He said to him, 'You shall love the Lord your God with all your heart and with all your soul and with all your mind. This is the great and first commandment. And a second is like it: You shall love your neighbor as yourself.'" (Matt. 22:37–39)
. . . for our sanctification . . .	"In him we have obtained an inheritance, having been predestined according to the purpose of him who works all things according to the counsel of his will . . . ." (Eph. 1:11) "And we know that for those who love God all things work together for good, for those who are called according to His purpose. For those whom He foreknew He also predestined to be conformed to the image of his Son . . . ." (Rom. 8:28–29)
. . . and to glorify you more.	"So, whether you eat or drink, or whatever you do, do all to the glory of God." (1 Cor. 10:31)
Grant us wisdom and grace to train and instruct our children in the Lord.	"Fathers, do not provoke your children to anger, but bring them up in the discipline and instruction of the Lord." (Eph. 6:4) "If any of you lacks wisdom, let him ask God, who gives generously to all without reproach, and it will be given him." (James 1:5)

The Prayer	Scriptural Basis
We plead for you to save them, according to your will and timing.	"But God, being rich in mercy, because of the great love with which He loved us, even when we were dead in our trespasses, made us alive together with Christ—by grace you have been saved . . . ." (Eph. 2:4–5) "Brothers, my heart's desire and prayer to God for them is that they may be saved." (Rom. 10:1) "No one can come to me unless the Father who sent me draws him. And, I will raise him up on the last day." (John 6:44)
We ask you to have mercy on them, in spite of their folly and our failures.	"Folly is bound up in the heart of a child, but the rod of discipline drives it far from him." (Prov. 22:15) "If you, O LORD, should mark iniquities, O Lord, who could stand? But with you there is forgiveness, that you may be feared." (Ps. 130:3–4)
Help us to keep remembering your character and your promises.	"O Lord God of Hosts, who is mighty as you are, O Lord, with your faithfulness all around you." (Ps. 89:8) "May grace and peace be multiplied to you in the knowledge of God and of Jesus our Lord. His divine power has granted to us all things that pertain to life and godliness, through the knowledge of him who called us to his own glory and excellence, by which he has granted to us his precious and very great promises, so that through them you may become partakers of the divine nature, having escaped from the corruption that is in the world because of sinful desire." (2 Peter 1:2–4)
Help us to live a holy life as we parent, in our minds/ hearts, and in our actions and reactions.	"Therefore, preparing your minds for action, and being sober-minded, set your hope fully on the grace that will be brought to you at the revelation of Jesus Christ. As obedient children, do not be conformed to the passions of your former ignorance, but as he who called you is holy, you also be holy in all your conduct, since it is written, 'You shall be holy, for I am holy.' " (1 Peter 1:13–16) "For the eyes of the Lord run to and fro throughout the whole earth, to give strong support to those whose heart is blameless toward him." (2 Chron. 16:9)

The Prayer	Scriptural Basis
Help our delight and joy to be in Christ, even during the times we may sorrow.	"I am speaking the truth in Christ—I am not lying; my conscience bears me witness in the Holy Spirit—that I have great sorrow and increasing anguish in my heart. For I could wish that I myself were accursed and cut off from Christ for the sake of my brothers, my kinsmen according to the flesh." (Rom. 9:1–3) "As sorrowful, yet always rejoicing; as poor, yet making many rich; as having nothing, yet possessing everything." (2 Cor. 6:10) "Then I will go to the altar of God, to God my exceeding joy, and I will praise you with the lyre, O God, my God." (Ps. 43:4) "For you, O Lord, are my hope, my trust, O Lord, from my youth." (Ps. 71:5)
Give us grace to do what is right even if others or our children do not understand.	"For am I now seeking the approval of man, or of God? Or am I trying to please man? If I were still trying to please man, I would not be a servant of Christ." (Gal. 1:10) "And God is able to make all grace abound to you, so that having all sufficiency in all things at all times, you may abound in every good work." (2 Cor. 9:8)
Help us not to be proud but to humbly depend on your help and pursue the prayers and help of other Christians.	"I am the vine; you are the branches. Whoever abides in me and I in him, he it is that bears much fruit, for apart from me you can do nothing." (John 15:5) "Whoever isolates himself seeks his own desire; he breaks out against all sound judgment." (Prov. 18:1) "Clothe yourselves, all of you, with humility toward one another, for 'God opposes the proud but gives grace to the humble.' Humble yourselves, therefore, under the mighty hand of God so that at the proper time he may exalt you, casting all your anxieties on him, because he cares for you." (1 Peter 5:5–7)

The Prayer	Scriptural Basis
Lord, we do trust your sovereignty, wisdom, goodness, and faithfulness.	"For my thoughts are not your thoughts, neither are your ways my ways, declares the LORD. For as the heavens are higher than the earth, so are my ways higher than your ways and my thoughts than your thoughts. For as the rain and the snow come down from heaven and do not return there but water the earth, making it bring forth and sprout, giving seed to the sower and bread to the eater, so shall my word be that goes out from my mouth; it shall not return to me empty, but it shall accomplish that which I purpose, and shall succeed in the thing for which I sent it." (Isa. 55:8–11) "The Rock, his work is perfect, for all his ways are justice. A God of faithfulness and without iniquity, just and upright is he." (Deut. 32:4) "And those who know your name put their *trust* in you, for you, O Lord, have not forsaken those who seek you." (Ps. 9:10, emphasis added)
We look forward to seeing how you are going to work in our lives and our children's lives, and to the opportunities that you will give us (and possibly our children) to glorify you.	"Now to him who is able to do far more abundantly than all that we ask or think, according to the power at work within us, to him be glory in the church and in Christ Jesus throughout all generations, forever and ever. Amen." (Eph. 3:20–21)
Thank you again for the blessing of our children, and most of all, for all of the blessings that we have in you.	"Oh give thanks to the Lord, for he is good, for his steadfast love endures forever!" (Ps. 107:1) "Every good gift and every perfect gift is from above, coming down from the Father of lights with whom there is no variation or shadow due to change." (James 1:17)
In Jesus' Name, Amen	

Appendix A:
Presenting the Gospel in Its Context: Faithfully Sowing the Seed according to the Scriptures

STUART AND ZONDRA SCOTT

I believe the greatest desire Christian parents have for their children is that they come to a saving knowledge of the Lord Jesus Christ. However, parents must be sure that this desire does not become their personal parenting goal rather than faithfulness to the Lord, for his glory. Only God can do the work of salvation. Our children's trust in Christ must be their own personal response. So, we must trust God and relinquish the desire to control as we faithfully teach the gospel truths about Jesus to our children. This outline is a tool to assist parents in teaching the context and key elements of the glorious gospel of the Lord Jesus Christ. Out of the great desire to see children come to faith, it can be tempting to abbreviate the truth or call them to a response prematurely. The outline is not an exhaustive study, but a guide that parents can use in the sharing of gospel truth to their children. From the moment a child can hear, parents can teach them about the nature and acts of God from the Scripture.

The kernel of the gospel is found in 1 Corinthians 15:3–4, "that Christ died for our sins in accordance with the Scriptures, that he was buried, that he was raised on the third day in accordance with the Scriptures." The phrase "in accordance with the Scriptures" is repeated to give the all-important context of who Christ was and is, why he came and why he died, and the importance of his rising from the dead.

Another helpful reference is found in Acts 16:30–31 where the Philippian jailer said to Paul and Silas, "Sirs, what must I do to be saved?" And they said, "Believe in the Lord Jesus, and you will be saved, you and your household." Well, that wasn't enough of the Gospel for the jailer to either embrace or reject Christ. The next verse (16:32) tells us that Paul and Silas then instructed the man and his household in "the word of the Lord to him and to all who were in his house." More of the Gospel truth was needed and then God graciously saved them. In our efforts to share the gospel with our children we want to make sure that it is given in its context and flows with the themes of Scripture: God and eternity past, creation, the fall, redemption, the church, new heaven and new earth.

One part of the outline that can be especially helpful for children reared in Christian homes is that containing the 2 Corinthians 5:15 passage (VIII, B, 2c). Children who grow up hearing the gospel, but God does not grant them grace to believe, can become familiar with the words, make emotional and self-serving "decisions," and not be saved—thus "the Christianized pagan." It is important for the child to consider whether he is habitually living for self or Christ. This section of the outline can help parents highlight for their children that if they have true saving faith in Christ, then they will have a new desire and ability to live habitually (although imperfectly) for Christ and not for self.

Parents can pray for wisdom in deciding what to teach at any given time, keeping instruction appropriate to the age of the child. Remember, there is not one gospel for children and another for adults. The Scriptures encourage adult-like content and child-like faith, not the other way around. The challenge is to put that content as much on their level as possible without compromise. We must trust that the Spirit will *supernaturally* enlighten the heart of the one (even a child) whom he is drawing (John 6:37–44).

May God bless you as you seek to be faithful in presenting the gospel of the Lord Jesus Christ to your children.

I. Understanding God—Part 1: A Few Specific Attributes

   A. There is no one like the one true God—Deut. 4:35; Ps. 86:8, 10; Isa. 40:18, 25–26; 44:6–7a; 46:5, 9.

   B. He is triune (three distinct persons, of one substance, different in function)—Gen. 1:26; Deut. 6:4; Matt. 28:19; Luke 3:21–22; John 1:1, 14; 5:18; 10:30; Acts 5:3–4; 2 Cor. 13:14; Col. 2:9; 1 Thess. 1:2–5; 1 Peter 1:2.

   C. He is the creator, and he is personal —Gen. 1:26; Ps. 95:6–7; 100:3; Isa. 44:24; John 16:14; 17:1, 4,

22–26; Acts 17:24–25; Col. 1:16–17 (". . . through him and for him.")

D. He is almighty and sovereign—Deut. 32:39; Ps. 24:1–2; 47:7–8; 103:19; 135:5–6; Isa. 46:9–11; Rom. 1:20; 8:28–29.

E. He is eternal—Isa. 57:15; Col. 1:16–20; Jude 24–25.

F. He is righteous and holy—1 Sam. 2:2; Ps. 5:4; Isa. 6:3; Hab. 1:13; 1 Peter 1:14–16; 1 John 1:5; Rev. 4:8.

G. He is just—Deut. 32:4; Ps. 9:7–8; 89:14; Acts 17:31; Gal. 3:10; 1 Peter 3:18.

II. Understanding Man as Originally Created before the Fall

A. Created in God's image to worship God, delight in him, reflect his glory, live for his advantage, and proclaim his majesty—Deut. 10:12–13; Ps. 16:11; 73:25–26; Isa. 43:6–7; Col. 1:16–18.

B. Created to be loved, cared for, blessed by, taught by, satisfied by, and comforted by God, and to walk with him—Gen. 1:27–30; 2:15–17; 3:8; Ex. 6:7; Deut. 4:20; Ps. 100:3: 107:8–9; Isa. 30:18; 43:4; Ezek. 14:11; John 4:24; 14:22–23; Titus 2:14.

III. Understanding Sin—Breaking or Not Keeping God's Law

A. Sin began with Satan in heaven—Gen. 3:1–15; Isa. 14:12; Luke 10:18; 2 Peter 2:4; Jude 6.

B. Sin on earth began with Adam and has been passed to all mankind—Gen. 2:17–18; 3:1–7; Rom. 3:23; 5:12, 18.

C. We are responsible individually for choosing to sin—Eccl. 7:20; Isa. 53:6; Ezek. 18:2, 20; Rom. 3:23; Gal. 3:10; Eph. 2:1–3.

D. Sin separates—Gen. 3:8–24; Isa. 53:6a; 59:2; Titus 3:3.

E. God's wrath is upon all the unsaved—Ps. 5:4; Prov. 15:8–9; John 3:36; Rom. 1:18.

F. Death, judgment, and hell are the results of our sin—Ex. 34:6–7; Ps. 7:11; Matt. 10:28; 13:38–42, 49–50; 25:31–46; Acts 17:30; Rom. 6:23; Gal. 3:10; 1 Thess. 1:10; Heb. 9:27; 10:26–27; Rev. 20:11–15.

G. Mankind has been totally depraved since the fall of Adam—Jer. 17:9–10; Rom. 3:10–18; Eph. 2:1–3; 4:17–19; Titus 3:3.

IV. Understanding Our Hopelessness apart from God's Grace

A. Not by nature can we be righteous—Eccl. 7:20; Isa. 53:6; 64:6; John 1:13; Rom. 3:10–18.

B. Not by works—Eph. 2:8–9; Phil. 3:1–10; Titus 3:4–7; James 2:10.

C. Not by heritage or lineage—John 1:13; Phil. 3:4–7.

D. Not by our own will—John 1:12–13; 6:44, 65; Phil. 3:9.

E. Our debt is insurmountable—Ps. 130:3; Matt. 18:21–35; Luke 7:40–50.

F. No hope—Rom. 2:2–3; Gal. 3:10, 22–24; Eph. 2:12; Phil. 3:1–10; Col. 3:5–6; 1 Thess. 4:13.

V. Understanding God—Part 2: More Specific Attributes[1]

   A. He is merciful and compassionate—Ex. 33:19; Ps. 36:5; 145:8–9; Isa. 63:9; Lam. 3:31–33; John 1:14; 2 Cor. 1:3; 1 John 4:8.

   B. He is all-wise—Isa. 55:8; Rom. 11:33–34.

   C. He is gracious in two ways:

     1. His common goodness—Matt. 5:43–48; Rom. 2:4.

     2. His salvific (saving) grace for the elect—John 6:37, 44, 65; Rom. 9:15–16; Eph. 1:3–6; 2:4–7; 1 Thess. 1:4.

   D. He is angry with the wicked, yet loving at the same time—Ps. 5:4; Prov. 15:8–9; John 3:16; 1 John 3:16; 4:8–10; Mark 10:17–22.

VI. Understanding the Incarnation

   A. The God-man—John 1:1, 14; Mark 10:45; Phil. 2:5–11.

   B. Jesus' life: 100 percent righteous—2 Cor. 5:21; Heb. 4:15.

   C. Jesus' death: paid in full for our sin; removed God's wrath; imputed Christ's righteousness for believers—Rom. 5:19; 2 Cor. 5:21; Gal. 3:13–14; 1 Peter 3:18.

   D. God the Father was satisfied with Christ's death—Isa. 53:10–11.

   E. Jesus' resurrection: power over death and hope to come—1 Cor. 15:3–4; 1 Peter 1:3–5.

1. These are only a sampling of the attributes of God. For further reading, see Arthur W. Pink, *The Attributes of God* (Grand Rapids: Baker, 1991).

F. God offers reconciliation by grace through faith in Christ—Acts 17:30–31; Rom. 6:23; 10:13; 2 Cor. 5:18–19; Eph. 2:13.

G. God declares believers to be justified through Christ—Rom. 3:24–26.

H. God offers forgiveness of sins and heaven to believers only through Jesus—John 14:1–6; Acts 4:12; Col. 2:13.

I. God seeks worshipers and a people for himself through Jesus—Isa. 45:22; John 4:23; Eph. 1:4.

VII. Understanding Saving Faith ("believing")— John 1:12; 3:16

A. The knowledge (content) of the gospel, with Jesus as the object of faith—John 17:3; Heb. 6:4; 10:26; James 2:19.

B. The agreement (intellectual assent) with the gospel facts—Matt. 13:20; John 6:44, 65; Acts 26; Heb. 6:4; James 2:19.

C. A personal transfer of reliance from oneself to Jesus alone for justification—Isa. 55:6–7; Matt. 13:23; Luke 14:25–33; John 14:21; Acts 3:19; 11:18; 2 Cor. 5:15; Phil. 3:9; 1 Thess. 1:9; 2 Tim. 2:25–26. This involves godly sorrow and repentance for all sin, an about-face and an all-out pursuit to love, submit to, fully trust in, and follow after the Lord Jesus Christ in obedience to his revealed will, by the Spirit's enablement (grace, Acts 11:18; 2 Tim. 2:25). This saving faith will always result in good works (Eph. 2:10; James 2:26). Faith and repentance are the only evidences that a man has a new heart: turning from sin to Christ reveals a new heart; failure to turn from sin and to Christ reveals an old heart.

VIII. Coming to Christ

    A. Not in the wrong way—Matt. 7:21; 19:16–22.

        1. Doing God a favor that is deserving of his grace—"I'm so special."

        2. Only for fire insurance (to avoid hell at death)—"I don't want to suffer forever."

        3. Adding a good and helpful thing to my life—"Why not, it can't hurt?"

        4. So I can go to heaven with my family—"I want to see and be with them."

        5. Wanting to become a better person—"I'm already good and this can make me better."

        6. So Jesus can give me what I want, but I'm still living for my advantage.

        7. Wanting to be saved "in my sin" and not "from my sin."

    B. But in the right way

        1. With the right attitude

            a. Humbled with a broken and contrite heart over my sin before a holy God—Matt. 5:3–5; Luke 15:18–19; 18:13–14.

            b. Overwhelmed by God's undeserved goodness—Rom. 11:33–36.

        2. With the right intentions—Jesus Christ as Lord.

            a. With a true desire and determination to turn from my sin and from living for myself—2 Cor. 5:15; 7:9–11; 1 Thess. 1:9.

    b. With a true desire and determination to depend on Christ's righteousness and to live for him—2 Cor. 5:15; 1 Thess. 1:9.

    c. To whose advantage ("for" whom) am I living? 2 Cor. 5:15.

       i. World—Rom. 12:1–2; 2 Cor. 10:5; 1 John 2:15–17.

       ii. Sex—1 Cor. 7:1; 1 Thess. 4:3–8; 1 Tim. 5:1–2.

       iii. Work—Col. 3:23–25; 2 Thess. 3:6–9.

       iv. Future—Matt. 6:33; James 4:15.

       v. Church—1 Cor. 12:12, 25; Eph. 4:11–13; Heb. 10:24–25.

       vi. Bible—John 14:21; 1 John 5:2–3.

       vii. Appearance—1 Sam. 16:7; 1 Peter 3:3–4.

       viii. Others—Rom. 12:9–13; 2 Cor. 5:18–20; Gal. 5:13.

IX. Understanding Our Reconciliation with God—2 Cor. 5

    A. He has given us a new heart—Ezek. 11:19–20; 36:25–27; 2 Cor. 5:17.

    B. God reconciled us (his elect) to himself — 2 Cor. 5:17–18; Eph. 1:4; 1 Peter 3:18.

    C. He is our God, and we are his people—Rom. 9:23–26; 1 Peter 2:24–25; Rev. 21:3.

    D. He is our shepherd, high priest, comforter, and guide—Ps. 23; John 10:27–28; 2 Cor. 1:3–4; Heb. 4:14–16.

    E. We are to be his ambassadors to others—Matt. 28:19–20; 2 Cor. 5:18, 20.

F. He will take us home (by death or by his return)
    to live with him, whom we eagerly await, and
    worship him forever—John 14:1–3; Col. 3:1–4;
    1 Thess. 1:9–10; Rev. 22:1–3.

X. Warning to Those Who Reject the Gospel

A. Because of unbelief—John 3:36; 5:24;
    1 John 2:19.

B. Because of abandoning the only hope—
    John 14:6; Acts 4:12; Heb. 6:4–8; 10:26–31.

C. Their way is treacherous—Prov. 13:15;
    Heb. 3:12–19.

D. They will never experience what a life of worship-
    ing God is like—Matt. 19:16–22; John 10:10.

E. They will be separated from God and his grace
    forever—Rev. 20:12–15; 21:8.

You may order the PowerPoint presentation of this appendix on CD-ROM from www.scottresourcesforhim.com. See
Martha's and Stuart's web sites for other helpful resources for
troubled kids. Martha's Web site is www.marthapeace.com.

Appendix B:
"Put Off"/"Put On"
Dynamic

MARTHA PEACE

This Bible study is for teaching Christians how to deal practically with their sin. Many times we are aware that we need to make changes in our lives, and we confess the appropriate sins to God. However, we may find ourselves committing those same sins again and again. Habitual sin is especially difficult because we automatically respond wrongly, without thinking. Therefore, it is important to learn exactly what God has to teach us through his Word about establishing new habit patterns.

Before you begin this study, pray and ask God to show you the truth of his Word. Now begin by looking up the following Scriptures and write out answers to the questions.

1. How do we become aware of sin? Heb. 4:12; John 16:7–8.
2. Do we *have* to sin? Explain. See Rom. 6:6, 7, 14.
3. Describe the "old self." See Eph. 4:22.
4. Describe the "new self." See Eph. 4:24.
5. What are we to "put off" and what are we to "put on"? See Eph. 4:22, 24.
6. What are we to "put off" (lay aside), according to Col. 3:9?
7. What are we to "put on," according to Col. 3:10?
8. This "new self" is to be renewed. How? See Col. 3:10.

Thus, we see that we are to "put off" our old ways of thinking and acting, and "put on" new ways that are like those of Jesus Christ. When sinful ways of thinking or responding have become habitual, confessing that sin is not enough. The sinful habit pattern must be *replaced* with a righteous habit pattern. It is as if what we "put on" is the biblical antidote to what we "put off." For example, it is not enough to just stop telling lies. A person must work at telling the truth, the whole truth. By God's help (grace) he will become a truthful person.

Look up the following Scriptures and fill in the chart:

Scripture Reference	"Put Off" Character Deficiencies	"Put On" Character Qualities
1. Eph. 4:25		
2. Eph. 4:26 – 27		
3. Eph. 4:28		
4. Eph. 4:29		
5. Eph. 4:31– 32		
6. Eph. 5:4		
7. Eph. 5:11		
8. Eph. 5:18		
9. Phil. 4:6		
10. Col. 3:8, 12– 14		
11. Rom. 13:12–14		

As we have seen, God gives Christians the Holy Spirit to convict them of sin and to help them carry out God's desires. As a result, is there anything that God requires that a Christian cannot do? See Philippians 4:13. God will never ask us to do something that he will not give us the grace to carry out. Sometimes we may not feel like obeying God; however, if we do obey (in spite of our feelings), God will give us grace.

1. Write down specific sins in your life that you know need to be "put off."
2. Take time now to confess these sins to God.
3. Write down what you are to "put on" (biblical antidote) in your life in the place of these sins.
4. Write down some practical actions you can do to "put on" godly character.
5. Based on what you have learned in this study, write out your prayer.

Appendix C: The Making of a Man of God

PHIL JOHNSON

"From childhood you have been acquainted with the sacred writings, which are able to make you wise for salvation through faith in Christ Jesus." (2 Tim. 3:15)[1]

Charles Spurgeon is unique in the annals of church history. He had no university or seminary degree. He was known for his preaching, not his scholarship. And yet he left a body of published work that represents the most prolific individual output of any well-known Christian in history. Over the past century and a half he has influenced millions of pastors and laymen for good. His books, primarily collections of sermons, are still in print and selling as briskly as ever. The current resurgence of Calvinism owes in part to his continuing influence.

1. This article is used with the permission of the author.

A Precocious Child

Charles Spurgeon was born in a little cottage in Kelvedon, Essex, on June 19, 1834 (ten days after William Carey died in India). His father and grandfather were both pastors.

Eighteen months later, when his mother was about to deliver a second child, little Charles was sent to visit his grandparents in nearby Stambourne. Apparently mother or newborn suffered some long-term illness or complication, so the boy's stay in his grandparents' home was extended, then extended some more. Spurgeon did not return to live with his own parents until he was six.

The arrangement worked well for all. James Spurgeon loved having his eldest grandson by his side, and often took the toddler with him on pastoral visits. In the providence of God, those years of bonding with his grandfather set the course for Charles Spurgeon's life.

Charles was a gifted child who began reading early. He loved his grandfather's Puritan library. At first it was the leather covers that interested him the most, but soon he found the books themselves a rich source of wisdom and interest. It was from his grandfather's library that he obtained his first copy of *The Pilgrim's Progress*, and that book became his lifelong favorite. Before the age of ten, he was reading and comprehending some of the richest theological works that have ever been written.

Spurgeon was precocious in other ways, too. By the time he returned to his parents' home, he already had three younger siblings, and the six-year-old was deeply conscious of his responsibility to influence them for good. This unusual maturity was surely the legacy of his grandfather's example. It became a persistent trait in young Charles. Even before he reached his teens, his hobbies were writing poetry and editing a magazine. He was already honing the literary skills that would make him legendary. Shortly before his conversion at age fifteen, he wrote a 295-page book called *Antichrist and Her Brood* or, *Popery Unmasked.*

Look at Spurgeon in any stage of his development and you will see someone wise beyond his years, with an exceptionally mature outlook on life. Spurgeon himself made reference to this. At age forty, he lectured on "Young Men" and referred to himself as an *old* man:

> I might have been a young man at twelve, but at sixteen I was a sober, respectable Baptist parson, sitting in the chair and ruling and governing the church. At that period of my life, when I ought perhaps to have been in the playground, developing my legs and sinews, which no doubt would have kept me from the gout now, I spent my time at my books, studying and working hard.

Spurgeon is sometimes erroneously portrayed as a careless unbeliever who was suddenly converted to Christ when he walked into a church almost by accident. Nothing could be farther from the truth. Christian influences had shaped him from the time of his infancy.

A Burdened Sinner

When Spurgeon was ten, he began to be deeply convicted by the realization that he had no saving knowledge of Christ. He set out on a quest for salvation that was to last five years. It was an agonizing time of life for him. He took spiritual matters far more seriously than the typical youth. The knowledge that he was not a true Christian was a heavy burden that was perpetually at the forefront of his consciousness.

Here's what Spurgeon himself wrote about those dark years of conviction:

> When I was in the hand of the Holy Spirit, under conviction of sin, I had a clear and sharp sense of the justice of God. Sin, whatever it might be to other people, became to me an intolerable burden. It was not so much that I feared hell, as that I feared *sin*; and all the while, I had upon my mind a deep concern for the honour of God's name, and the integrity of His moral government.

Despite his upbringing in a pastor's home, and although he never succumbed to any kind of gross, life-destroying sin, Spurgeon nonetheless retained until the end of his life a very keen sense that he was a horrible sinner. Even though he was converted at a fairly young age, Spurgeon described himself as one of those "who were kept by God a long while before we found Him." In his mind, those years of bearing the load of his own sin were an eternity, and he retained the fresh memory of that guilt until the end of his life.

Spurgeon later wrote of the awful turmoil he experienced during that time:

> Day and night God's hand was heavy on me. If I slept a night I dreamed of the bottomless pit . . . . God's law was flogging me with its ten-thonged whip and then rubbing me with brine afterwards, so that I did shake and quiver with pain and anguish.

Conversion came through unlikely circumstances. One Sunday morning, while Spurgeon was desperately seeking salvation, a terrible snowstorm virtually shut down the little town of Colchester. It was January 6, 1850, and the snowstorm grew worst just as Spurgeon began to make his way to church. He turned down a side street and ducked into a *different* church, a tiny Primitive Methodist chapel, where a service was just under way with no more than fifteen people in attendance.

Apparently the regular pastor couldn't get through the blizzard that morning, so a reluctant and inarticulate layman finally got up to deliver the morning sermon. The man was obviously inexperienced and unprepared. He chose for his text Isaiah 45:22: "Look unto me, and be ye saved, all the ends of the earth: for I am God, and there is none else."

After reading the text, the man began his exposition: "Now lookin' don't take a deal of pains. It ain't liftin' your foot or your finger; it is just, 'Look.' Well, a man needn't go to college to learn to look. You may be the biggest fool, and yet you can *look*."

Spurgeon said the man couldn't even pronounce some of his words correctly, and he ran out of material within a few minutes. Then, fixing his eyes on the one conspicuous visitor in the place, he said directly to Spurgeon, "Young man, you look very miserable." Then he added at the top of his lungs, "Young man, look to Jesus Christ. Look! Look! Look! You have nothin' to do but to look and live."

Spurgeon said, "I saw at once the way of salvation. . . . I had been waiting to do fifty things, but when I heard that word, 'Look!' what a charming word it seemed to me!"

The burden was immediately lifted, and Spurgeon was filled with a joy he had never known. "I thought I could dance all the way home. I could understand what John Bunyan meant when he declared he wanted to tell the crows on the plowed land all about his conversion. He was too full to hold. He must tell somebody."

The Prince of Preachers

The following year Spurgeon transferred to a school in Cambridge, joined a Baptist church there, and preached his first sermon in a house meeting. His preaching gift was immediately evident, and he was soon asked to fill the pulpit of a small church in Waterbeach, six miles from Cambridge. He promised to preach only a few Sundays, but he ended up remaining there for more than two years. Those circumstances made it impossible for him to pursue any more formal education.

But his fame as a preacher quickly grew, and in December of 1853 he was asked to candidate at the New Park Street Baptist Church, the largest and best-known Baptist congregation in London. Its historical pulpit had been occupied in previous generations by John Gill, Benjamin Keach, and John Rippon—all Baptist legends. Although the country boy felt awkward and out of place in the large city, the congregation warmed quickly to his preaching and soon called him to be their pastor.

And so exactly five years and one day after his conversion, Spurgeon preached his first sermon as pastor of the congregation he would shepherd for almost forty years until the day he died. He was soon preaching weekly to crowds numbering 10,000 and more. (He once preached without amplification to a crowd of nearly 24,000 in London's Crystal Palace.) Under his ministry, the New Park Street Church outgrew their facility and built the famous Metropolitan Tabernacle in the heart of south London. Membership under Spurgeon's leadership exploded from 232 to 5,300.

More than 25,000 copies of Spurgeon's printed sermons were sold weekly. The sermons were compiled in 63 thick volumes that are still being published today. They comprise some 25 million words.

Spurgeon never attended an hour of seminary. He seems to have sprung full-grown into maturity as a preacher and theologian. But the truth is that there were many circumstances arranged by Providence that made Spurgeon what he was.

There was his father's and grandfather's influence, of course. And there were all those Puritan works he began reading as a child. Spurgeon had an incredible, nearly photographic memory, and he could read a book once and remember years later exactly where to find a section he wanted to quote. Into his life as a Christian he drew with him an encyclopedic knowledge gleaned from a childhood of intense interest in spiritual things.

One other profound influence on Spurgeon should be mentioned. In the autumn before his conversion, he attended a private school in Cambridgeshire. The cook and housekeeper there was a woman named Mary King. Spurgeon often said afterward that he was indebted to her for much of his theology. She enjoyed talking theology, and in Spurgeon she found a kindred spirit. She was a strong Calvinist who loved the doctrines of grace. Spurgeon said he "learned more from her than . . . from any six doctors of divinity of the sort we have nowadays."

A number of factors combined to make Spurgeon the great preacher we remember. But what stands out most remarkably is that the foundation of his ministry was established in his childhood years. He stated near the end of his life that after forty years of ministry, he hadn't moved an inch from the convictions he held when he began his ministry. To a large degree, that was because such a solid character and such strong convictions were shaped by so many wonderful childhood influences.

Phillip R. Johnson is executive director of Grace to You and curator of the Spurgeon Archive (www.spurgeon.org), the Internet's largest collection of Spurgeon resources. From John MacArthur, *Biblical Parenting for Life* (Sun Valley, Calif.: Grace Community Church, 1998, 2000).

Appendix D: Taking Thoughts Captive

STUART AND ZONDRA SCOTT

"[We] take every thought captive to obey Christ" (2 Cor. 10:5). See also Rom. 12:2; 2 Cor. 11:3; Eph. 4:23; Phil. 4:6–9; Col. 3:1–2, 16; 1 Thess. 5:17.

In chapters 3 and 8, the authors write about wrong thinking by parents in regard to rearing their children. Here is a work sheet that can help you to examine your thinking and bring it back on track by taking your thoughts captive for Christ. We are to renew our minds with the Scriptures (Rom. 12:2), and this is generally done one thought at a time. As you use the L.O.R.D. pattern to renew your thoughts, be sure to pray for God's help and to *directly* relate each step to your void of God and to each untrue and sinful thought. Also be sure to ask God to help you to refocus on who God is, His blessings, His will, and his perspective. This work sheet is a tool to assist in the renewal process.

- What was the original circumstance/stimulus/temptation that brought about your wrong thinking, and your response (include feelings, thoughts and actions)?

_____

_____

_____

- What were the basic thoughts that needed change or addition?

_____

_____

_____

- Take one thought at a time, by using the L.O.R.D. response pattern found in Phil. 4:6–9. The key elements covered in Phil. 4:6–9 can be formed into the acronym L.O.R.D. (Lift Up, Offer, Renew, and Do).

_____

_____

_____

L—I will *lift up* my heart in prayer "with thanksgiving" (v. 6); cf. Ps. 100:4.
Lord you are: _____
I am thankful for: _____
You have done: _____

O—I will *offer* my humble request: "by prayer and supplication . . . let your requests be made known to God" (v. 6). "Lord, considering this situation, I would like to ask you for . . . .": When you bring requests to God, be sure to keep

your concerns in order of priority:(1) God's will/glory/
help, (2) others' well-being, and (3) my desires.

_____

_____

_____

R—I will *renew* with your truth: "whatever is true . . . honor-
able . . . just . . . pure . . . lovely . . . commendable . . . [excel-
lent], worthy of praise—*think about these things*" (v. 8). "Lord,
in this situation I will study what you say about my thought
(commands or teachings related to the topics of the original
circumstance or response)":

Topic / Scripture

_____

_____

_____

"Lord, in this situation I will remember that you promise":

Promise/ Scripture

_____

_____

_____

"Lord, in this situation I will recognize, confess, and repent
of any sinful/untrue/godless thinking."

_____

_____

_____

My new biblical thought: "Lord, I will *willfully* rehearse this new thought before and at the time that this situation and/ or wrong thinking arises again":

_____

_____

_____

Is it absolutely factual? Is God and his truth in it? Is it thankful, hopeful, trusting? Is it profitable? Is it focused on God (and others if applicable)? Does it glorify God? Is it void of sin, self-focus, bitterness, vengeance, discouragement, and regret?

D—I will *do* what is helpful and right: "practice these things" (v. 9).

- "Lord, I will (to help this situation and/or follow through on scriptural principles) make practical and righteous plans of the things I must do (be specific and concrete):

_____

_____

_____

- "Lord, I will acquire accountability, prayer, and encourage-ment for these things (if needed) from (name):

_____

- Lord, I will ask for and depend on your strength and power to renew my thoughts.

It will be very helpful to commit the L.O.R.D. response pat-tern to memory.

240

Martha Peace (RN, Grady Memorial Hospital School of Nursing, Atlanta; BSN, Georgia State University, Atlanta) is a Bible teacher and nouthetic counselor to women through the Faith Biblical Counseling Center at Faith Bible Church, Sharpsburg, Georgia. She conducts seminars for women on topics such as "The Excellent Wife," "Becoming a Titus 2 Woman," "Personal Purity," "Having a High View of God," and "Raising Kids Without Raising Cain." She is the author of six books including *The Excellent Wife* and *Damsels in Distress*. Martha worked for eight years as a counselor to women at the Atlanta Biblical Counseling Center. Her work experience also includes six years as an instructor for women's classes at Carver Bible College and Institute in Atlanta, and thirteen years as a registered nurse. She is an adjunct faculty member at The Master's College. She and her husband, Sanford, have two grown children and twelve grandchildren.

Stuart W. Scott (BA, Columbia International University; MDiv, Grace Theological Seminary; DMin, Covenant Theological Seminary) is an associate professor of biblical counseling at Southern Baptist Seminary in Louisville, where he has taught for five years. Prior to coming to Southern Seminary, Scott served on the faculty of The Master's College and Seminary in biblical counseling. He has over thirty years of pastoral experience, including eight years as an associate pastor at Grace Community Church in Sun Valley, California, with Pastor John MacArthur. He is a fellow and member of the board of the National Association of Nouthetic Counselors (NANC). As author of *The Exem-*

plary Husband and several booklets, he continues to work on materials for family and counseling issues. He and his wife, Zondra, enjoy traveling, the outdoors, and spending time with their adult children, Christa and Marc, and their grandchildren, River and Isabella.